WHAT WOULD Henry DO?

Essays for the 21st Century

Volume II

Published by Thoreau Farm Trust Inc.,
a 501(c)(3) corporation, dedicated to preserving
the house in which Henry David Thoreau
was born on July 12, 1817.

Edited by
Executive Director Rebecca Migdal, Thoreau Farm trustees Molly Eberle,
Nancy McJennett, and Ken Lizotte, and
former Executive Director Margaret Carroll-Bergman

Cover and interior design by Cindy Murphy, Bluemoon Graphics

Cover photos by Nancy McJennett and Ryan Owen

Crayon drawing of young Henry on front cover: Samuel Rowse,
"Henry David Thoreau," William Munroe Special Collections
at the Concord Free Public Library.

Available at your local bookshop, Amazon.com, Barnes & Noble, the
Thoreau Society bookstore at Walden Pond or direct from Thoreau Farm.
Bulk orders of ten or more copies available at a 10% discount
when ordered from Thoreau Farm.

Thoreau Farm, 341 Virginia Road, Concord Massachusetts 01742
www.thoreaufarm.org • info@thoreaufarm.org

ISBN-13: 979-8838858603
ISBN-10: 8838858603

Independently published

Dedicated to the residents of Concord and
to the Town of Concord, our partners in
preserving the birthplace of Henry David Thoreau

Thoreau Farm Trust Board at Walden Pond, May 2022
(front row, left to right) Ken Lizotte, Joseph C. Wheeler, Jack Maguire
(back row, left to right) Peter Alden, Nancy McJennett,
Nicole Palmer, Molly Eberle, Court Booth
Absent from photo: Lawrence Buell

THOREAU FARM

BIRTHPLACE OF HENRY DAVID THOREAU

Contents

Senator Edward J. Markey

Foreword

Senator Edward J. Markey

If Mr. Thoreau and I were to meet, I suspect we would have some disagreements. Given the chance, I would especially like to press him on his assertion in "Civil Disobedience" that "no man with a genius for legislation has appeared in America." I would not claim that I am a genius or that all 500 pieces of legislation I have passed in my career contain the moving eloquence and philosophical insight that Mr. Thoreau possessed, but surely, Henry, some must be worthwhile? Perhaps he would challenge the whole premise of being a Senator — after all, he did famously pronounce "I accept the motto 'the government is best which governs least.'" Upon further consideration, "disagreement" could be an understatement.

Still, in Thoreau's work I see an abiding patriotism — a love for the United States that expressed itself in the belief that it could always be made better, that together it was our responsibility to push our nation toward justice. Thoreau published "Civil Disobedience" in 1849, when the embers that would ignite into the Civil War were already smoldering. He was a staunch abolitionist, delivering lectures against the Fugitive Slave Law and establishing the Thoreau family home in Concord as a safe haven on the Underground Railroad. During this time, he also saw the expansion of factories that exploited their workers and polluted the waterways of Massachusetts he so loved. These experiences led him first to "Civil Disobedience" and eventually to *Walden*, a founding text of the American environmental movement. Any critique Thoreau levied against the United States emerged from a deep love of nature and his fellow people, sown with the knowledge that both must be cherished and protected. He

believed in service. He believed in the sacredness of the Earth.
He believed in people.

I have spent my life fighting for the same ideals. For Thoreau —
and for me — the environmental movement is a political struggle,
rooted in the push for justice for our people and for our planet.
That struggle only becomes more vital with each passing year. As
when Thoreau wrote "Civil Disobedience," the moment is dire.
Scientists agree that we have entered a climate emergency, and
that climate change will continue to cost us lives and livelihoods
if we fail to respond with the scope and scale this crisis demands.
Our responsibility to act is undeniable.

If Thoreau were alive today, I am confident he would be standing
on the front lines of the climate movement, working with me,
with our young people, and with the communities most harmed
by environmental racism and injustice. He would be our partner
in passing transformative climate legislation and building a
more just, sustainable future. He would likely have a few choice
criticisms of our government — and perhaps even dispute the
"genius" of our legislation — but I know he would approach the
cause of environmental justice with the same fervor, intellect, and
love he devoted to Walden Pond. I would be grateful to count
him as an ally.

Thoreau's last words were "Now comes good sailing." To the end,
he believed in the promise the future held — if we are prepared
to fight for it. Right now, our planet is in crisis. But the work we
do today will help create the better world we know is possible.
Let us move forward together, guided by the principles and
values of our nation that Thoreau helped shape: sustainability,
justice, liberty, and equality. Let us advocate for a future that is
more prosperous and more peaceful for our Commonwealth, our
country, and our world. Now is the time, this is the place, and we
are the people.

Senator Edward J. Markey *is a consumer champion and national leader on energy, environmental protection, and telecommunications policy. He has a deep commitment to improving the lives of the people of Massachusetts and our country. After serving 37 years in the U.S. House of Representatives, he was elected to the Senate in 2013.*

Following Thoreau's legacy, Ed has been a fierce advocate for our environment and for communities harmed by pollution, climate change, and environmental injustice. He is the co-author of the Green New Deal alongside Congresswoman Alexandria Ocasio-Cortez, which sets in place a 10-year mobilization to achieve a green economy, taking into account every community and prioritizing environmental justice for all. He was a leading voice in the investigation into the BP oil spill, and in 2009 was the co-author of the landmark Waxman-Markey bill, the first comprehensive climate legislation ever to pass a chamber of Congress. He was also the principal House author of laws to increase fuel economy standards and stop the construction of hundreds of coal-fired plants. Simultaneously, Ed was the leader of the national Nuclear Freeze movement, banning all underground nuclear testing and spearheading efforts to prevent the spread of nuclear weapons.

Ed was born and grew up in a blue-collar neighborhood in Malden, Massachusetts, where he still lives. He attended Boston College and Boston College Law School, and is married to Dr. Susan Blumenthal.

Photo credit: Rich Morgan Photography

Ken Lizotte, *CMC, is President of the Board of Trustees at Thoreau Farm and Chief Imaginative Officer (CIO) of emerson consulting group inc., which transforms business experts and their firms into "thoughtleaders," similar to the thoughtleadership model developed by Ralph Waldo Emerson and Henry David Thoreau. Author of eight books, Ken lives in Concord with his family and their Golden Retriever, Beckett.*

Introduction: NOW What Would Henry Do?

Ken Lizotte

It's been five years since our first volume of *What Would Henry Do?* Perhaps you have noticed a number of, let's say, "distracting" things that happened since then. I could list them all but that strikes me as redundant because we all know what they are. With this second edition, we at Thoreau Farm again pose the question of our book's title to more than 40 new volunteer essayists. As president of Thoreau Farm's Board of Trustees, it falls to me to sort out my own thoughts in an introductory essay. To help me collect such thoughts, I've added a word to begin the question, with emphasis: NOW what would Henry do?

Where to start? How do we make sense of the many unseemly (to be kind) political maneuverings that assail us every day, or the ravages of a worldwide pandemic that has so far left untold millions dead, the horrors of the current war raging in Ukraine, and so forth? What should we think, say, and do about all of this? I must admit I am somewhat at a loss.

Then it dawned on me: Why struggle all by myself to figure out what to write? Why not locate the source itself? That is ... Why not ask Henry himself to weigh in?

Finding him at first wasn't easy as I hadn't seen him around Concord in a while, though he used to be a daily fixture hustling through the village, even during his two years, two months, and two days at Walden Pond. But I did have his cell number (yes, he actually loves cell phones, see Maria Madison's essay in Volume I), so I sent him a text. To my pleasant surprise, he texted me right back! "Colonial Inn for lunch tomorrow?" it read. "My family used to live there."

The next day, he was there at exactly noon, waiting for me at an outdoor table. His appearance was a little different than when I had last seen him, spectacles now framing tired eyes, a zippered forest green Patagonia vest to keep him warm, a very, very, very tattered copy of Darwin's *Origin* (a treatise he found literally exciting) on the table before him.

Additionally, he sported a yellow & blue N95 mask while seeming to be in some kind of reverie, staring up at the day's cumulus clouds. I had to hail him as I approached to get his attention.

"Hulloo!" he replied, holding up his right palm as the Algonquins, Concord's first residents, did. "Always a pleasure to dine under the whitest of clouds on a sunny day. Fluffy castles in the air."

I complimented him on his mask of Ukrainian flag colors, to which he replied, "Once again, war and destruction have come our way. I've been working on an essay about it for The Roost. I have to go on record."

We ordered lunch, a cheeseburger, well done, for me, a black bean burger for Henry. "I can no longer abide consuming animals," he said. "All life needs to be respected, especially in these times."

He was not agitated or surly, however, as I recalled he could be in earlier days. Instead, he seemed somewhat at peace in a way I was not used to. So it felt safe to ask him straight out what he thought about the world today and let him take it from there.

"I've been isolating a lot lately," he began, "more even than when I lived in my place at the pond. The lockdown has given me permission to just keep to myself, which I prefer. So I'm thinking, writing, rewriting, reflecting. Conclusions are hard, recommendations even harder. I can't claim I've put many thoughts into action. But I *have* been thinking."

He ran through a litany of potential follow-up actions to all this reflecting: actually going to Ukraine to help the refugees, as he'd done for the Underground Railroad. Or offering himself to missions like Dr. Goodall's, which aim to protect today's all-too-many endangered species. Finally, of course, there was climate change, an urgency, he sighed, "that just won't go away."

We talked his confusion out a bit and then I shared my own. As a writer myself, I too, struggled with moving from the abstraction of ideas to outright action. Gradually, after a dessert of Indian pudding (his suggestion), we experienced a Spockish melding of minds, i.e., if writing was something we both knew we could do, that was our logical first step. From writing, inspired action would follow.

This seemed to buoy Henry. He was sitting up a little straighter now, eyes energized and peering up at the sky again. He even shared an atypical smile. "How I wish Waldo were here with us," he mused. "He was a master at this sort of thing."

I paid the check despite his quiet protest that he had planned to do so. "I just completed a three-week surveying job," he explained cheerily. "So, I'm feeling filled with silver dollars." But then he added a kind of confession. "Our talk has been fruitful for me. It has inspired me to go back to my hideaway now and write more about these important matters. Then tomorrow, I think I will call the Goodall institute and volunteer to help. Anything they need, I will do." There was gratitude in his tone.

As he sauntered away down Monument Street in the direction of the Old Manse, walking still his favored mode of transportation, I realized Henry's pathway to thinking, saying, and doing was no different than for us all. Think and reflect, speak/say (perhaps by writing), then take whatever necessary action feels rightest. Actions might change day to day, but thinking a thing through was the key to getting moving.

Meanwhile, I made my way back toward Concord center, passing the site of the original meetinghouse where Henry once vigorously and publicly denounced the arrest of John Brown. Looking up at those "whitest of clouds" that he had delighted in, I recognized that today was indeed a sunny day as he had proclaimed, bright, positive, fresh, and filled with great hope.

Featured Q & A

Dr. Jane Goodall

Photo by Vincent Calmel

Dr. Jane Goodall

How to Save Our "Glorious Living Tapestry"

Dr. Jane Goodall

Thoreau Farm: Henry David Thoreau was an observer of and friend to animals, birds, fish, insects — all living things. What would Henry think, say, and, most importantly, do about the danger of extinction in our time?

Well, he would most certainly be shocked, saddened, and angry. I suspect he would make use of modern technology to reach out to people in other countries. Although he never travelled further than Canada, he read about the travels and explorations of others, including Darwin and Humboldt. He was fascinated by the natural world and the spiritual impact of being in nature, so surely he would be upset to see the loss of biodiversity around the world. He would share his love of the natural world in stories for the children he taught and perhaps see the value of spreading his love wider through social media.

TF: Many people today say social media is a breeding ground of intolerance, divisiveness, and other negative behaviors. Yet you have included social media in your listing of "reasons for hope," saying: "It is by acting together, in this exciting way, that we can involve thousands — millions — of people, and this is what is going to change the world." What is your opinion on this?

Social media in and of itself is neither good nor bad. It depends on how we use it. The more people who want to protect and restore the natural world and who understand our place in it and our responsibility towards it, the more will want to use social media for the good of the planet. As long as social media exists, there will be people using it for the wrong reasons, and the more important it becomes for more and more people to use it for the right reasons.

Part of Hitler's propaganda was "If you tell a lie often enough, people will believe it." Many dictators share that belief. But it must also be true that "If you say a truth often enough, it will be believed." I think Thoreau might have felt the same, but I don't really know.

TF: You have said: "When you live in the forest, it's easy to see that everything's connected." When did this insight first hit you — your first day or week in the forest or sometime afterward? And what event or observation suddenly drove this insight home to you?

I only understood this after I had been in the forests of Gombe for some time. At first, I was so desperate to gain the trust of the shy chimpanzees and to find out about their behavior that I had no time to understand the interconnectedness of all the species of animals and plants. It was later, when I was on my own — perhaps waiting for chimpanzees to arrive in a fruit tree — that the forest began to speak to me. For then I had time to watch the behavior of birds and insects and see how they depended on the trees and plants. I realized it was like a glorious living tapestry, and that if a species disappeared, it would be as though a thread were pulled from that tapestry. And if enough threads were pulled, then the tapestry would hang in tatters; the ecosystem would collapse. It was an understanding that came gradually as I became more spiritually connected to the forest around me.

TF: Thoreau was known to spend literally hours just watching ants carry on with their activities and learning from them, a commitment that many (maybe most) of us would not have patience for. What qualities do we need to cultivate to pay more attention to animals and other species in the wild?

Of course, patience is important, and that comes with curiosity, a passion to understand. To answer the 'Why?' and 'How?' questions. I was born loving animals and when I was just four years old, I waited, so I'm told, for some four hours in a hen house, for a hen to come in and lay an egg. Because no one would tell me where the hole was that was big enough for an egg to come out. My first real experience of what it takes to be a good observer of the natural world. Without doubt, it was the same curiosity that led Thoreau to spend hours watching ants.

TF: Where are we making progress in eradicating poaching and trafficking of great apes? It still feels like there's so much to do, so much animal cruelty still happening. What do you imagine Henry would do?

Indeed, there is so much to do. We are working on raising awareness, strengthening the equipment of the rangers who are protecting the national parks and reserves, educating people in the countries that are buying chimps for pets or entertainment, explaining the cruelty involved, the killing of the mothers. And continuing to raise the awareness of people everywhere that all the animals being trafficked are individuals, all can feel happy, depressed, fear and, of course, pain. Some groups in JGI are working on strengthening law enforcement.

TF: Your website states: "We emphasize local participation in conservation planning and monitoring, leverage mobile mapping technologies to provide communities with accurate information for conservation planning and management, and always strive to include local culture and community needs in our conservation approach." How much resistance do you encounter to these approaches and how do you overcome it?

In 1986, there were six groups of scientists studying wild chimpanzee behavior — in Tanzania (two groups), Uganda, Sierra Leone, Cote d'Ivoire, and Guinea Bissou. I helped organize a conference in Chicago to bring researchers together from those sites. During a session on conservation, I was shocked to see the extent of habitat destruction and decrease in chimpanzee numbers. I knew I had to try to do something to help. I managed to visit five countries within the chimps' range and learned a good deal about the chimps' plight. At the same time, I was also learning about the plight of so many people living in and around chimpanzee habitat. The crippling poverty, lack of good education and health facilities, the degradation of the land.

In 1960 when I began research in Gombe, the national park was part of the equatorial forest belt. By the late 80s Gombe was a tiny island of forest. All around were bare hills. Too many people living there for the land to support, too poor to buy food elsewhere, struggling to survive. They were cutting down the trees to make money from charcoal or timber, or to clear land to grow food for their growing population. That's when it hit me: "If we don't help the people find ways of living without destroying their environment, we can't save chimps, forests, or anything else."

In 1994, with a small grant from the EU, we (JGI) began Tacare (Take Care), our method of community-led conservation. To begin, we chose a team of local Tanzanians to go into the 12 villages around Gombe and ask what we could do to help. From the start, Tacare was designed as a holistic program — no good educating girls if they got sick from lack of good hygiene, no good restoring fertility to overused farmland (without toxic chemicals!) unless there were good water management programs. And so on. People came to trust us. We worked to improve schools and clinics. We introduced GIS, GPS, and satellite-imaging technology. We set up microfinancing programs so that people could start their own environmentally sustainable businesses, provided scholarships for girls, so they had a chance of secondary education, held family planning workshops, and trained volunteers to use smart phones to monitor the health of their village forest reserves.

We met almost no resistance: the village leaders and the local and central governments were supportive. The program now operates in 104 villages throughout the range of chimps in Tanzania — and also in six other African countries where JGI works with chimpanzees. Understanding the 'services' the forest provides, the villagers know that protecting the environment is not only for wildlife, but for their own future. They have become our partners in conservation.

TF: Many predict that it is already too late for us to reverse the destructive effects of climate change. Can the same be said for protecting great apes and other endangered species? How might Henry join you in this struggle?

I have a feeling that Henry would agree that we have a window of time when, if we get together, we can slow down climate change and loss of biodiversity. As we protect forests, so we protect apes, monkeys, and all the other plants and animals that live there. I hope Henry would join us by contributing to our program for youth, from kindergarten through university, Roots & Shoots. The young people choose projects to make the world a better place for people, animals, and the environment. Maybe he would provide stories to share with them, help them understand that we are actually part of the natural world, and depend on it for food, air, water — everything. But we depend on healthy ecosystems. We want children to spend time in nature so that they can learn to understand, come to love, and thus, want to protect it.

TF: We want to ask you about the Planet of the Apes movies! Would you consider them a positive or negative in terms of their portrayal of apes?

By and large I think they gave a good portrayal. I especially loved the first one, where the researchers were put into the very cages in which they had confined the chimps. The most recent, with Caesar, gave a very good message, although I disliked the Hollywood ending with all the violent warfare scenes.

TF: The fact that elephants too are in trouble today, with only 400,000 left vs.12 million just over 100 years ago, displays a crisis beyond apes and any one or two species. What can individuals do about that? The number of caring organizations to support is overwhelming. How can we choose whom to support and how? What might Henry do?

All you can do is careful research, check what percentage of donations go into the field versus administration, read about the results obtained — and choose the NGO that works with the environment or animal that you are most passionate about. So long as human populations and their livestock continue to grow, the environment will suffer. Animals and humans will run out of space and increasingly come into conflict with each other.

As he did in relation to corporal punishment, slavery, and so on, Henry could speak out passionately about the corruption and illegal criminal cartels that traffick the animals. And he could collaborate with JGI and help us spread the message that we need to get together and act NOW. That each one of us makes a difference every day, and we can choose what kind of difference we make. That millions of ethical choices in how we live each day will cumulatively make a powerful impact. And I'm sure he would help us promote the idea that we should all spend time in nature, especially small children.

Dr. Jane Goodall *is known for groundbreaking studies of wild chimpanzees in Gombe Stream National Park, Tanzania, which forever changed our understanding of our relationship to the rest of the animal kingdom. This transformative research continues today as the longest running wild chimpanzee study in the world. Dr. Goodall's work builds on scientific innovations, growing a lifetime of advocacy including trailblazing efforts through her international organization the Jane Goodall Institute which advances community-led conservation, animal welfare, science, and youth empowerment through its Roots & Shoots program.*

Today, Dr. Goodall continues to connect with worldwide audiences, despite the pandemic, through "Virtual Jane," which includes remote lectures, recordings, and her podcast, the Jane Goodall Hopecast. In 2021, she was the recipient of the Templeton Prize, and her newest book, The Book of Hope: A Survival Guide for Trying Times, *was published.*

A global icon, Dr. Goodall has always dedicated herself to the spreading of actions that create hope and a meaningful positive impact toward a better world for people, other animals, and the planet we share.

Photo credit: Sherry Stewart 2017

Carol Travis Alonso *is a physicist, author, and horsewoman. She was a co-discoverer of Element 106, Seaborgium, with Nobel laureate Glenn Seaborg and other team members in Berkeley, California. During her long scientific career, Carol maintained a deep interest in history and her own creative writing. Her book* Sun Stallion *(2019), a historical novel of the Conquest of Peru, was a finalist in the 2018 Blazing Lantern Fiction Contest. Recently, she published* Simplicity, Simplicity — 101 Poems Based on Henry David Thoreau's Walden. *Reflecting Henry's most poetic and thoughtful observations, the poems are accompanied by vintage pen-and-ink sketches. Carol's other passion is dressage — the art of dancing with horses. She has won numerous awards in her specialty, freestyle to music.*

The Gift of History

Carol Alonso

"Three thousand years and the world so little changed."
— Henry David Thoreau, *Journal*, March 3, 1838

Thoreau's greatest gift to us is his perception that, during all history, human nature has not changed. Young Henry recognized that Virgil was describing the same details of nature that Thoreau studied every day on his walks. He was not alone. His best friend was a Roman.

Reading history further led to Henry's conviction that human nature — the human mind — is and has been essentially the same in all ages and places. *When* an event happens is not so important, because all ages are equal.

The similarities between people, even those of widely different times, places, or races, far outweigh their differences. "The permanence of nature and of human nature — the equivalence of all eras" gives hope to us all.

This liberated Henry because it meant that we — with the right attitudes and aspirations — can be as noble and achieving as the Greeks and the Romans. Americans had an equal chance of becoming great thinkers and achievers.

(As an aside, Henry would adore the timeless classic Chinese poetry translated by Vermont's David Hinton. It is as soothing as a glass river, flowing unceasingly over time, unchanged over millennia of human war and famine, plenty, and sorrow. "Nothing has changed. Nothing will change.")

Emerson taught Thoreau to "shape his own life and pursue his own ends." Henry became a Stoic: one should live one's own life, turning not to a god or a state or a society but to Nature to define one's individual self.

So, Henry lived and thought apart, and abjured the normal trappings of society. He communicated via thoughtful letters and personal conversation, believing that careful thought should precede his actions. He tried to respect other opinions, if grounded by truth and logic.

How would Thoreau communicate today? He would love his computer but not own a television. He would disengage from Facebook and most social media. Henry would be an intellectual activist but never join a group of violent protesters. And he would beware of false news.

Henry, who knew the dangers of false news, avoided reading newspapers. Charles Dickens, visiting America in 1842, was horrified by our corrupt newspapers. Henry and Charles would be even more aghast at today's inaccurate Web information, which is capable of transforming society.

For Henry, society was the means for individual self-fulfillment. Today, the overpopulation of our planet and country has hugely increased social pressures. Henry would remind us that we should not become what others wish us to be; we should be ourselves. To quote Steve Jobs, "Don't live someone else's life."

Henry would urge us to stay in touch with our country and our world, and "at the least do not impose on your fellows." But at the same time be self-reliant. Do not expect your society to take care of you. Believe that individualism can be the best means of social reform.

Human nature may not have changed over the eras, but science and technology have changed human experience. In many ways modern humans have been unable to adapt responsibly to some technological advances, including guns and social networks.

One positive scientific development involves DNA. Charles Darwin published *The Origin of Species* in 1859, just three years before Thoreau died. How excited Henry must have been to read it, because his studies of nature convinced him there was some unifying mystery underlying all life forms. Now we know that a vast number of identical genes are shared by all animals, from salamanders to humans. Thoreau and Darwin, visiting today, would be totally astonished.

For Americans in today's tumultuous times, as for Henry, our personal efforts to come to terms with our own times depend on how we honestly view the past, as well as our own life experience.

So, Henry would probably give us this final advice: embrace the pain, and the glory, of accurate history. Do not rewrite it to meet your own ends. History teaches you who you are, and who you can be. It provides the great comfort that you are not alone. History is our greatest hope and a precious gift.

Cal Armistead *is the author of* Being Henry David, *an award-winning young adult novel. She has written for* Shape Magazine, The Chicago Tribune, The Christian Science Monitor, *and other publications. Armistead lives and writes in Acton, Massachusetts, a mere 10-minute drive from Walden Pond.*

What Would Henry Tell the Teens of Today?

Cal Armistead

It was a steamy day in May, and I was at the Thoreau Farm for a solo writer's retreat. As I sat at a replica of Thoreau's small green desk from Walden in the room where Henry David drew his first breath in this world, I struggled to get my bearings.

I'd heard stories of how writers have sensed the encouraging spirit of Henry as they worked. Although I'm a student of his writing and life, I couldn't say I knew Thoreau well enough to speculate on what his spirit would think of me inhabiting his birth room nearly 205 years after the event.

In fact, I found it hard to imagine Thoreau as an infant at all. Surely, he had sprung to life fully formed, like Athena from the head of Zeus, as the beloved philosopher, writer, and naturalist we know today. Yet, long before that, he was a helpless infant squalling in his mother's arms, and these walls were the first to echo the sound of his voice. I peered out the window at a spring-lush oak tree, clutched my notebooks and pens to my chest, and appealed to the ether for inspiration.

It came when I imagined Henry as a toddler, a child, and then a teenager. Ah, a teenager. That was my "in." I'd written a contemporary novel for teens in 2013 titled *Being Henry David*, featuring Thoreau as a spirit guide for my protagonist. I was at the Thoreau Farm that weekend to begin work on a sequel.

Although the modern concept of adolescence didn't exist in the early 1800s, no doubt Henry himself suffered from awkwardness,

5

acne, and angst like any other teen. He must have asked himself: Who am I? Where do I belong? What is my purpose?

Life for a teenager today is strikingly different from in Thoreau's day, yet Henry must have felt growing pains and moments of quiet desperation like anyone else, then or now. He wouldn't have arrived at his later wisdom if he hadn't in younger years lost his way, his grounding, his sense of self.

Thoreau's forays into the wild allowed him to delve more deeply into what it was to be fully alive and part of the greater whole. The more he learned and the closer he drew to nature, the more he seemed to know himself.

"It is in vain to dream of a wildness distant from ourselves," he wrote. "There is none such."

And furthermore, "I believe there is a subtle magnetism in Nature, which, if we unconsciously yield to it, will direct us aright."

Is Henry suggesting we seek direction from nature when we're lost, scared, and disconnected? This certainly appears to be What Henry Would Do. But how do we do the same?

I interpret Thoreau's "subtle magnetism" that will "direct us aright" as akin to what some call the still, small voice within. It's that internal knowing that can only be accessed if we slow down, are quiet, and listen. (Deliberately.)

What better place to consult it than steeped in nature?

Perhaps this is what Henry would recommend. Step One: Immerse the self in a natural environment, preferably in solitude, that most companionable of companions. Step Two: Be still and silent, because "Silence is the communing of conscious soul with itself." Step Three: Engage the senses. "I see, smell, hear, feel, that everlasting Something to which we are allied, at once our maker, our abode, our destiny, our very selves…" Step Four: Recognize that each of us is nature. The stuff of nature is the stuff we're made of, every precious cell and molecule and freckle and eyelash. "I love and worship myself with a love which absorbs my love for the world." Step Five: Yield to the "subtle magnetism in Nature." Learn to hear the abundant wisdom nestled in the unconscious.

Repeat as necessary.

I think of this as a critical lesson that is just as true now as in Thoreau's day, not just for struggling teens in search of identity and meaning, but for everyone.

What Would Henry Do? He'd say: Look to Nature as your guide and compass. She will show you the way home, to yourself.

Bonnie Beaudet *is a licensed Concord Tour Guide, a docent at Thoreau Farm, and a staff member of the Concord Visitor Center. She grew up 10 miles east of Walden Pond and now lives 10 miles west of Walden Pond.*

An Authentic Life

Bonnie Beaudet

The Pond glistens as a gentle breeze caresses its surface. A ripple appears in the water in front of me and I wonder if the fish know I am here. Some people look for me at Sleepy Hollow Cemetery but there you will find only my bones. The wise come to the Pond for it is here that my spirit soars.

This is the place where I found my voice. This is where it all began for me. After my brother, John, died I was quite lost. I was not myself for a long while and my mother and dear sisters feared they would lose me, too. Then my good friend, Waldo, bought a woodlot on this spot and I asked if I could build a house in which to write. As generous as ever, he said "yes." So, I borrowed the axe of another friend and began the next phase of my life.

In truth I came here as much to grieve and to hide as I did to write. After the accidental fire that burned 300 acres of forest, I was ridiculed. "Woods burner," they called me. Fortunately, I was with the son of Judge Hoar when this happened. He was able to make peace with the townsfolk and we were not prosecuted. They did not know how much it pained me to see those tall, proud pine trees burn. I grieved for them as I grieved for John.

Today I am called the father of the environmental movement though I was not much for movements. I believed that if each individual acted according to his or her own principles the world would be a better place. I stand by that even now, for I cherished my individualism.

When I moved to the Pond, I was a young man. Though I lived here for only two years, two months, and two days of my nearly 45 years on Earth, many define me by that period.

I left these woods not because I grew weary of this place but because I had more lives to live. By the time my book was published, seven years after I left my little house, I was no longer the same young man who had lived at the Pond. My thoughts had evolved and crystallized and I went through many drafts before I was ready to release my words to the world.

It amuses me that people think they know me. If you read my journals you will see that my views changed through the years. It was a different person who lived at the Pond than the one who met John Brown and ranted about the injustice of slavery. I was criticized for not being consistent, but to live is to change, and knowledge brings new perceptions. I was forever learning, so I was forever changing. You cannot put me in a box and say I was this or I was that throughout my life. I would be embarrassed if that were so, for it would mean that I was static and rigid.

The world with its new inventions and technology constantly brings more ways to communicate and educate. Evolution and progress require that attitudes be adjusted. In my writing I sometimes used the word "savages" to refer to Indigenous People. I would be shamefaced to use that word today and your omnipresent social media would crush me. Indeed, I would not use certain words if writing today, but I meant no injury when I used them in my time.

That my words are still relevant astonishes me. If I walked among you today, I would likely say or write something deemed politically incorrect and be "canceled." It is, in that way, a more dangerous world than it was in my day.

But I say to you, do not be afraid. Go confidently forth, sharing what insights you can. Some will understand, others will not. Do not fear criticism nor hold too tightly to preconceived notions. As new information emerges, your views and opinions may change.

They should change. It means you are paying attention. It means you are learning. It means you are growing. It means you are living an authentic life.

Margaret Carroll-Bergman *is the former executive director of the Thoreau Farm Trust. She is an award-winning journalist, who lives in a 575 sq. ft. house with her husband, Keith, on White Pond in Concord, Massachusetts. Their adult children visit in shifts.*

The Journals of Thoreau's Long-Suffering Lifetime Companion

Margaret Carroll-Bergman

"Time is but the stream I go a-fishing in," Thoreau wrote. So, let's imagine him, his domestic partner, who calls him by his last name, and friends, living in the present day.

July 12

T.'s birthday! I thought I'd surprise him with a new shirt, but he said, "… beware of all enterprises that require new clothes…" and put on his favorite "surveying" shirt, the same shirt he's been wearing all month.

July 30

T's mother dropped by the cabin today. She doesn't think he is eating enough … always stopping by her house around meal time.

Of course, he's hungry all the time. He walks at least four hours a day!

October 2

What's the use of setting a mouse trap, if T. keeps springing it?

The mice are moving in for the winter. I ask T. for help in exterminating them, but he only captures one to later show to his naturalist friend, muttering something about it "… not [being one of] the common ones, which are said to have been introduced into the country, but a wild native kind not found in the village."

Honestly, I can't help but wonder about a man who says without a hint of irony, "...and when ... I held still a piece of cheese between my thumb and finger, it came and nibbled it, sitting in my hand, and afterward cleaned its face and paws, like a fly, and walked away."

Sometimes I think our cat, Min, has more sense than T.

October 12

T. had surveyed White Pond years before, and found it "perhaps the most attractive" of all our lakes, so we moved to Walden's lesser twin and have been living in a little cabin there for more than a decade. He believes micro huts are an elegant solution to the affordable housing crisis, not only here, but everywhere. "It's green and better for the planet, too," he said.

October 27

It's been a long time since we left Cape Cod, but the grey, damp day and the oily smell of fish that hangs in the air makes him nostalgic for the back shore. He picks up *Cape Cod*, and starts to dreamily read his favorite selections out loud.

November 3

Went on a mushroom foray with T. in Fairhaven. Much time was spent sauntering, which is a very slow (aggressively slow) pace. We didn't find any edibles, but T. stumbled upon what can only be described as a pornographic mushroom.

"Pray what was Nature thinking of when she made this? She almost puts herself on a level with those who draw in privies," he said, with a half-smile.

December 15

T. is meeting with Waldo today for advice. He's thinking about going into pencils with his father; there are 11 pencil factories here in town! Can Concord support one more? I think T. should stick to surveying and his spoken-word journals.

I also wonder if Waldo is the best person for any sort of advice. He exhumed his first wife — poor, dead Ellen — just to have a look at her, and asked his second wife — Lydia — to change her name to Lydian. And, she did!

Thank God T.'s no Waldo when it comes to relationships, but he is painfully honest.

It also helps that I can bake a blue-ribbon pie.

January 1

T. and I just got into our outdoor bath, when a few dozen people stumbled upon us, drunk from the night before, ready to take their Polar Plunge for the new year in the pond. Our cabin is small. We can't fit more than the custom-made twin bed, three chairs, and T.'s work-station, more or less a sink or a tub.

T.'s looking over my shoulder as I write this, reminding me that we entertained 25 to 30 people here not too long ago. He offers me a glass of Retsina. T. says the smell reminds him of pine needles. (It's as close to drinking turpentine as one can get.) Happy New Year!

M. Allen Cunningham *is an author, publisher, and teacher,
the editor of the book* Funny-Ass Thoreau, *and the creator of*
Thoreau's Leaves, *a podcast.*

A Few Good *Would Nots*

M. Allen Cunningham

From the spring of 1845 onward, Thoreau was an avid reader and exponent of the Bhagavad Gita.

Was he thinking of this passage in the Gita when he wrote this passage in *Walden*?

As the ignorant act with attachment to actions, Arjuna, so wise men should act with detachment to preserve the world.

Probably I should not consciously and deliberately forsake my particular calling to do the good which society demands of me, to save the universe from annihilation; and I believe that a like but infinitely greater steadfastness elsewhere is all that now preserves it

Thoreau's Bartleby-esque withdrawal, while often used as a premise to dismiss him, or bastardized to justify hippie self-indulgence and parasitism, nevertheless pervades *Walden*. The words above appear in his opening salvo, "Economy," the chapter where he lays out his logic of detachment with the greatest emphasis — and with a quality Robert D. Richardson calls "Hindu stoicism."

Thoreau is reflecting on the subject of doing good in the world. "What good I do, in the common sense of that word," he said, "must be aside from my main path, and for the most part wholly unintended." And with uncanny timeliness for anybody reading

him amid our global pandemic, he makes an epidemiology of his
objection to simply doing good:

"If I knew for certainty that a man was coming to my house with
the conscious design of doing me good, I should run for my life
[...] for fear that I should get some of his good done to me, —
some of its virus mingled with my blood. No, — in this case I
should rather suffer evil the natural way."

When I wonder what Henry would do in these, our roiling,
censorious, sanctimonious, and increasingly illiberal times,
my mind moves to his predilection for principled detachment.
Coexistent with his readiness to speak out — to rail against
conventionality, complacency, and injustice — Thoreau's
detachment is indeed more Hinduism (i.e., grounded in
philosophy and values), more Liberalism (i.e., grounded in free
thought and openness), than it is Bartleby-ism (i.e., reflexive,
inarticulate stubbornness).

In this respect I don't think it's a dodge to answer our question
by considering Henry's would nots.

To wit, even amid today's grave societal ills and the seriousness
of our civic unrest, Henry most certainly would not abide the
hysterical sameness of thought, and mob sentiments, that our
current media propagate.

Would not clad himself in the Justice League spandex of Twitter
or other social media.

Would not make Manichean speech bubble pronouncements or
coin meme-ifiable ad hominem assessments of anyone's goodness
or evil, complicity or innocence, victimhood or aggression, on the
basis of their immutable characteristics.

Would not hesitate to echo the imperative of Martin Luther King,
Jr., an American hero he directly inspired, that it is content of
character that matters most in our dealings with each other and in
our pursuit of the dream of justice.

Would not accept as true and right any grievances, positions, policy ideas, or movements whose claim to truth and rightness relies primarily on their currency in the culture and their appeal to the masses.

Would not espouse any ideology or unified movement — not any — of protest or politics.

Would not embrace tyranny by any majority, no matter how morally vivid and infallible the majority's claims or slogans might appear.

Would not forsake, in other words, his particular calling in order to conform to the particular "good" that society or any group might, in their own inflexible terms, demand of him.

He was a child of Concord, born mere miles from the site of the shot heard 'round the world, and for him the principle of liberty was always axiomatic. Liberty, for this stalwart of the Underground Railroad, was the clarifying idea upon which he undertook his own lifelong revolution — no less effectual for being counterintuitively solo. His particular calling was the study of nature (wildness was for him equivalent to liberty) and the distillation of his best thoughts upon the page — or at the lyceum. As I've said elsewhere, the Thoreauvian revolution is a matter of inward moral clarity at the level of the individual situated within the natural world, never a holy-minded movement en masse.

So, I believe Henry would maintain his individual abstention, his revolutionary but never silent detachment, and keep walking in the woods, keep striving to record in his journal his crystalline, reverberant perceptions and the core truths of his liberal conscience, keep deliberately living and bearing witness and speaking out to wake his neighbors up, to instill change by his own small example, beginning in his own little village.

"Men say, practically, Begin where you are [...] and with kindness aforethought go about doing good. If I were to preach at all in this strain, I should say rather, Set about being good."

Kevin Dann *is an historian, naturalist, troubadour, and author of 12 books, including* Expect Great Things: The Life and Search of Henry David Thoreau. *He's taught at Rutgers University, University of Vermont, and the State University of New York.*

Casting for Real Magic at Cattle-Show

Kevin Dann

"Surely, men love darkness rather than light."
— John 3:19, *King James Bible*

So concludes Henry Thoreau's astonishing September, 1860, address at the Middlesex Agricultural Society's annual fair, known to Concord region residents as "Cattle-Show." Cattle-Show had long been Henry's shorthand for the petty amusements of the mob, and as September was perennially the place and time of superficial spectacle, it was the perfect occasion for an extravagant display of Thoreauvian wisdom to kneecap the errant commonplaces of his neighbors. Shot through with self-deprecating wit and side-splitting word play, wrapped within this phenomenological penetration of the mystery of pine-to-oak forest succession, Henry performed his own dazzling sleight-of-hand in service of rock-bottom reality. Reality being in extremely scarce supply this September of 2021, I long to hear Henry utter a jeremiad that would shame us all out of our current perpetual state of Cattle-Show.

As America's and the world's youngsters trot off back to school this September wearing masks and navigating draconian mandates, their parents can be comforted that, should the next viral variant send them back into lockdown, the price of the 128 GB Oculus Quest 2 has fallen to just $299, and that among the newly available titles to play in "Augmented Reality" are: I Expect You to Die 2: The Spy & The Liar; Sniper Elite VR; Vader Immortal; and Until You Fall. If your 6th grader is squeamish about first-person-shooter virtual carnage, there is Real VR Fishing. No need for any Walden Pond, just pull on the VR gloves and goggles, and cast away in your living room!

If your kids are toddlers rather than teens, Cattle-Show has international YouTube star Blippi, a hyperkinetic adult clown keen to wildly gesticulate at life's mundane wonders — like fish. Don't expect even a virtual pond though, because orange-and-blue Blippi has a penchant for highly mediated — by monster trucks, backhoes, dirt bikes and other "fun" machines — encounters with Mother Nature. What child needs — or wants! — to visit an actual aquarium when you can watch Blippi point at sharks or sting rays while he sings "So many animals in the sea/ So many animals to see!"

America's agricultural fairs pioneered didactic demonstrations that mixed science and entertainment, often imitating the showmanship of the stage magician. Both Blippi's videos and cutting-edge AR and VR traffic in all the standard illusions of stage magic, relentlessly cross-cutting in hyper "Now you see it, now you don't!" mode. Cattle-Show gray magic has reached its apotheosis in the avalanche of digital edutainment that now saturates every child's surroundings. Every man was welcome to Cattle-Show, "even a transcendentalist," Henry asserted, so what would our transcendentalist at a contemporary Cattle-Show do to stay this cultural catastrophe?

Henry would go straight for the jugular, perhaps taking the very same tack that he took at the end of his 1860 tour de force. No doubt aware of the appearance of some sleight-of-hand behind his theory of forest succession, Thoreau playfully concluded his remarks with a series of magical allusions. He told of growing five yellow squashes weighing together 310 pounds, having for his "abracadabra presto-change" only performed "a little mysterious hoeing and manuring." He mused about the "perfect alchemists" who could transmute substances so, and ended in a prestidigital flurry calculated to summon his hearers away from theatrical illusion to transcendental truth: "Here you can dig, not gold, but the value which gold merely represents; and there is no Signor Blitz [a famous magician and ventriloquist] about it."

Two weeks after the address, poking about the artificial pond at Sleepy Hollow, he found small patches of water lilies established in the otherwise vegetation-less water. The lily-full river was nearly a half-mile distant, presenting a new seed mystery, which was answered for him by the presence of a few pouts and pickerel in the pond, who had transported the seed to the new environment. To undo the illusory magic of contemporary Cattle-Show, Henry would no doubt offer the flesh-and-blood reality of actual magic, the mysterious metamorphoses effortlessly performed by oak trees and squirrels, water-lilies and pout and pickerel. And by the human being, who is forever welcome to quit Cattle-Show for the wonders of Creation.

Kate Dike Blair *lives with her family near White Pond in Concord and is a core member of the Friends of White Pond, an advocacy group dedicated to preserving and protecting the water quality of the pond. She writes and edits articles for the Friends' newsletter,* Ponderings. *She is thrilled to report that an A-Pod, a machine which harvests algal blooms and converts them into fertilizer, will be at work on White Pond this summer. Kate is also a Hawthorne cousin by marriage. Her historical novel,* The Hawthorne Inheritance, *published by Sunbury Press in September 2021, explores the death of Nathaniel's younger sister, Louisa in the 1852 Henry Clay steamboat disaster.*

Henry's Gem of the Woods

Kate Dike Blair

Perhaps, in the summer of 1842, Henry accepted an invitation to sup in Concord with newlyweds Nathaniel and Sophia Hawthorne and Nathaniel's unmarried younger sister Louisa. Shy Henry worried, could this be a set-up? But no, their mutual friend Margaret Fuller, in town for one of Waldo Emerson's seminars, was also included. Louisa would need to travel many hours by stage from her home in Salem, and Margaret and Henry walk more than a mile from Waldo's house to Nathaniel's Old Manse. All would appreciate a swim on a hot, sticky day.

The five friends might have found their way to nearby Walden Pond, where, for modesty's sake, men swam on one side of the great blue expanse, and women on the other. Henry, by way of introduction to Louisa, stood on the shore of the pond and declaimed, "It is earth's eye, looking into which the beholder measures the depth of his own nature." His audience blushed before retreating to their designated bathing sites.

Refreshed, the group reconvened for a light repast upon Walden's shore. Henry entranced the women with tales of encouraging squirrels and woodchucks to come to his calls, and enticed Nathaniel to join him on his future limnology expeditions to the varied coves around the pond. "My data shows a decline in clarity and changes in temperature, and an increase in algal populations, and it worries me," he explained.

"Our uncle John is a member of several conservancy societies that protect and preserve Salem and its environs. Does not Concord have such organizations for its natural spaces?" inquired Louisa.

Margaret, familiar with local activism, replied, "Indeed, there are several church societies, but none specifically for ecological reasons. Perhaps our Henry should start one?"

"An excellent idea," agreed Henry. "Waldo owns much of the land around Walden, and I trust that he will keep it in good stead, and his descendants as well. I am more concerned with Walden's lesser twin, White Pond, a few miles west, named for its glistening sand with which my father finishes the pencils in his factory. I call White Pond my gem of the woods. It is one of many kettle ponds in peril as civilization progresses. I fear that the developments in these ponds' watersheds might one day lead to their deterioration due to the burgeoning of human activities and a dearth of conservancy."

"What would you have us do?" asked Margaret, always one to embrace a worthy cause.

Henry smiled at her enthusiasm. "As Louisa suggests, join an advocacy group, and convince the town and state to manage their kettle ponds' water quality, study problem drainage areas from the surrounding banks and shoreline, identify causes of nutrient loading by human activity, fishing, erosion, or agriculture, and mitigate any algal blooms mechanically or chemically..."

Margaret raised an eager hand. "What would be a mechanical mitigation for algae? Harvesting? Can we eat it?"

Henry gazed into Walden's crystalline waters. "I apologize. Sometimes my imagination runs away with me. Perhaps in the future someone will invent a machine that collects algal blooms and converts them into fertilizer. Just as I envision educational programs for children and adults to encourage responsible usage of the ponds and their environs, and foster coordination among the advocacy groups, government agencies, and individuals."

Henry stood and stretched. "But for now, we must begin our return journey before the midges swarm." As the friends packed up, Henry reminded them to leave no trace behind, and to tread lightly as they followed the path up the bank, in order to preserve the ecosystem of a pond that he so revered. "Ladies, lift your skirts. A careless sweep can do much damage to the delicate flora. Remember your personal responsibilities when we launch our conservancy group and petition the town and state to halt their progressive tactics."

"And if the town and state are not interested in cooperating?" asked Nathaniel, who tended to peer into the gloomier depths of society.

Henry's reply was sober, yet his eyes twinkled. "Sometimes, there is no other recourse than to be radical. But remember: If you must be disobedient, then at the very least, be civil."

James Earl *is a retired professor of English at the University of Oregon. He still serves as Director of the Insight Seminar program there.*

That Villages Were Universities

James W. Earl

Most people read *Walden* when they're in high school or college, when they're still too young to understand it. Students have so many other things on their minds that Thoreau hardly has a chance. That was certainly the case with me. I still have my copy of *Walden* from fifty years ago; marginal notes tell me I read about half of it, and half-understood that. It wasn't easy at that age to slow down, sit quietly, and listen attentively and respectfully to the thoughtful, reflective voice of someone long dead.

Teaching English for many years, I found ways to break through the youth barrier occasionally, to yank students out of their personal preoccupations long enough to give them a taste of adult genius. Many students decide almost instantly whether they like a book or not; if they've been told to read it, they almost inevitably don't like it. I don't mean to criticize students. I was one myself. But study is a bad word when you're young. Then for most of us education ends just as adulthood begins. We stop reading the great books just when we might begin to understand, enjoy, and profit from them.

I wouldn't want to criticize adults either, just because they're not reading Thoreau. It's not easy to find the time or the peace and quiet for reading of that sort. Besides, good reading is an art. It doesn't come naturally to most people. Like listening to classical music, it takes study and practice.

I think the university should finish what it starts. The questions posed by the humanities take on a new reality later in life, and our society doesn't offer much guidance after graduation day.

Of course we can learn all on our own; anyone can dabble in literature, history, philosophy, art, and music without a university. But there's no comparison between the random reading most people do and the sort of intellectual experience a university can provide.

Many people feel the university is elite, arrogant, out of touch with real people and real problems. With this in mind, a group of professors and townspeople at the University of Oregon in Eugene came together; they dreamed of an adult college, with demanding seminars on urgent and timely topics, taught by experts. At a certain stage of adulthood, study, despite its rigors, is not a bad word, but a welcome therapy. Montaigne says,

> *Old age puts more wrinkles in our minds than on our faces. We need a great provision of study, and great precaution, to avoid the imperfections it loads upon us, or at least to slow up their progress.*

Thoreau says much the same thing:

> *To read well, that is, to read true books in a true spirit, is a noble exercise, and one that will task the reader more than any exercise which the customs of the day esteem. It requires a training such as the athletes underwent, the steady intentional almost of the whole life to this object.*

Why work that hard? He explains,

> *There are probably words addressed to our condition exactly, which, if we could really hear and understand would be more salutary than the morning or the spring to our lives, and possibly put a new aspect on the face of things for us.*

Books can change our lives and renew our world — if only we know what and how to read. I can't say this as well as Thoreau:

> *It is time we had uncommon schools, that we did not leave off our education when we begin to be men and women. It is time that villages were universities, and their elder inhabitants the fellows of universities with leisure to pursue liberal studies the rest of their lives.*

At our university, in our college town, we put Thoreau's dream into practice. We established "Insight Seminars" for adults: affordable, non-credit classes on meaning-of-life topics in the humanities. We started with "The Art of Reading" and "The Aging Brain," then seminars on a hundred topics, including *Gilgamesh*, The Problem of Socrates, The *Meditations* of Marcus Aurelius, Augustine's *Confessions*, Understanding Islam, *The Bhagavad-Gita, The Tale of Genji, Don Quixote*, Montaigne's *Essays, War and Peace*, Gandhi, and many more — including, of course, *Walden.*

Will Eno *writes for theatre and television. He is a Pulitzer Finalist in Drama. Another essay on Thoreau appears in* Now Comes Good Sailing *(Princeton University Press, 2021). Among other projects, he is working on a television show set in Concord in the 1800s.*

The Present

Will Eno

It was probably hard to concentrate a thousand years ago. If you can live with mosquitos and thunder, you can probably live with cell phones. Maybe Henry David Thoreau would say something like this, if he could see the world we've insisted on since he died. He did write, after all, in the Conclusion of *Walden*, "Things do not change; we change." Maybe he'd say that all the beeping and screens and news, it's nothing new, it's just a fuller realization of the chaos and distraction our minds could always produce. Something compassionate and generous, like that.

Not that Thoreau was ever stingy or narrow, but there were times he might have held his view of the present moment a little more lightly, or expressed it in less-stark terms. He had a notion of it as something to be pursued and captured. But all moments are present moments, at some point or from some perspective, and our engagement with them, our willingness to live in them, is measured more on a continuum than with a Yes or No ledger. When you make the present moment into The Present Moment — unpredictable, grand, unrepeatable — and you bill it as a gateway to the eternal, you can make it almost too complicated to feel. And then, while we're busy asking too much of a little patch of time, we miss the diving peregrine falcon or the perfect song or the baby walking or whatever moment was the whole point of our paying attention in the first place. I hope an alive-today-Thoreau might adopt a more easeful conception of the present moment. If being dead can teach us anything, you'd hope it teaches us lightness and humility and how to relax.

One recent present moment was the televised landing of the Perseverance Rover on Mars, almost 200 million miles away. I watched in hard-to-explain tears, and asked my daughter Albertine to pause the cartoon *Scooby Doo on Zombie Island* and watch with me. It was so moving and mathematical, such an amazing feeling of travel, in the midst of one of the most homebound years most of us have ever known. "Find your eternity in each moment," Henry wrote in his journal on April 24, 1859. "Touchdown confirmed," Dr. Swati Mohan announced, on February 18, 2021. "Perseverance landed safely on the surface of Mars." An explosion of applause and cheers from Mission Control. A supportive "Cool," from Albertine.

For me, the moment was, if not perfect, at least completely full: my daughter; the Universe; applause and hollers after years of unknowing, hard work, and silence; American ingenuity and unity; and a children's cartoon. The presentness of the moment was spread across the Universe. It was happening on Mars, at Mission Control, on the couch, on the other end of the couch. The present moment for my daughter possibly included her dad, smiling and crying. And, maybe just as vividly, Daphne and Fred capturing a zombie, and Fred, assuming it was some local in a Halloween costume, trying to pull the mask off and instead pulling off the zombie's head, revealing that… *zombies are real.* Perseverance has landed. I hope I never forget all that, but I might. Memorability is not necessarily the same thing as truth or completeness or beauty. Life is fleeting in a few different ways, but we are given, by definition, a lifetime of moments to work with and build into something meaningful, real, and even possibly lasting.

What would Thoreau do, if he came around again? A lot, probably. In a way, there's no such thing as doing nothing. Almost surely, he'd remind us to simplify, to keep our old clothes while we reach for new ideas, to grab life and its moments by the horns. But maybe he'd also just be speechless for a while. If not speechless, at least quieted. At the incredible advances we've made, at the extent of the damage we've done, the reach of the new freedoms, the violence and intensity of the old inequalities. He might sit down for a while, let the moment be, maybe make a pencil. And then, having fully arrived, he'd somehow begin.

Brooklyn, NY
May 21, 2021

Ron Fein *is a Boston-area writer and public interest lawyer. His 2020 pandemic humor piece for* McSweeney's Internet Tendency *"Who's Laughing Now, Assholes? A Letter from Henry David Thoreau to Literature Faculties at Cushy Liberal Arts Schools" was among the site's most-viewed posts that year. Find him at ronfein. com and on Twitter @ronfein.*

"You Idiots Really Screwed This Up":
A Message from Henry David Thoreau on the Turning of the Seasons, Climate Change, and the Purple Bladderwort

Ron Fein

What in the ever-loving spirit of Nature have you dimwits done with the planet? My generation did some awful things, like invading Mexico and, you know, slavery. Also, one time out by Fairhaven Pond, I got loaded and started a forest fire.

But at least I didn't mess with the purple effing *bladderwort*.

That little aquatic plant *looks* delicate. But if you touch its bladders, they open and hoover up bugs and whatnot. The bugs are trapped and slowly digested for a long hellish death — much like being forced to take over your father's pencil business.

Those demon-blossoms used to be *everywhere*. In the summer of '58, I canoed up to Fairhaven Pond again. This time, I didn't start a fire, run into a tax collector, or (unlike that one time back in '54) find a dead body. What I did see were purple bladderworts *all over the frickin' water.*

Today? Well, purple bladderworts aren't extinct, but — much like affordable houses — you can't find any in Concord.

"Who gives a chap?" you ask. That's what my father would say, along with "come home and make pencils."

Here's the thing, Einstein: it's not just the purple bladderwort.

Canna lilies, fringed orchids, lady's tresses, and more: all gone, like the fifteen bucks I invested in Bronson Alcott's Fruitlands commune.

And it's all your fault. How do we know? *Science,* dog.

Back in '51, I needed scratch, and *fast.* I turned to the most logical option for a quick buck: a ten-year project of recording wildflower data, for a book on the seasons that surely would have sold millions if I hadn't died from consumption.

For eight years, I tromped around the woods and marshes, ignoring the old crones muttering "There goes Thoreau, the woods burner." I recorded the flowering dates of over three hundred species, careful to write in a near-indecipherable scrawl in case my journals fell into the wrong hands.

But recently, some professor in Boston found my journals, hidden inside old issues of *Pencilmakers Quarterly.* Dude then bushwhacked all over Concord looking for the same plants I recorded. (See, Pops? You can make a living at this without a side hustle running pencils.) It seems they now bloom two, four, sometimes *six* weeks earlier.

The flowers are confused as hell, because Concord's average April temperature is five degrees warmer than in my time. Look, I may have started a fire, but you dipsticks *heated the whole frickin' planet.* The plants that can't adapt are gone or on their way.

Don't care about flowers? Stuff this up your gullet: Walden Pond used to get two feet of solid ice, and wouldn't melt until early April. Today? Bro, a Massachusetts pond should not be ice free in *January.*

Now that you morons have scrambled the weather — a screwup on a scale not even Bronson Alcott could manage — it's going to get bad. You may not care about plants or pond ice, but you'll complain when mosquitoes bite your nacho-stuffed face during the Super Bowl. Then some Internet genius will suggest genetically engineering something to gobble up mosquito larvae.

Oh, you mean something like the *purple effing bladderwort?*

Yeah, you're screwed. But it's not too late for action.

"What would Henry do?" you ask. Well, I'd probably start a one-man protest, spend a night in jail, and get bailed out by my Aunt Maria. But here's what you should do.

I've already said "simplify, simplify," but every third car on the Route 2 rotary is a Lexus, so I'm not sure you're listening. Can you drive less? I once hoofed it all the way to *Fitchburg* just to make a point about a ninety-cent train fare.

Go solar. "Unfortunately, my roof isn't eligible." Okay — maybe your house, like mine, is made from shanty boards, chalk, and hair. But don't just stand there drooling; look up community "green power choice."

Call your elected officials — local, state, and federal. Not tomorrow — now.

Finally — no matter how deeply the pencil business may drive you into a life of quiet desperation — don't set the woods on fire.

John "Fitzy" Fitzsimmons *is a teacher, poet, songwriter, essayist and balladeer. He is called "a master of folk" by* The Boston Globe, *and praised as "an absolute treasure of American folksongs, stories and contagious charm" by Doris Kearns Goodwin. As "The Nobel laureate of New England Pub music"* [Globe Magazine], *Fitz has performed his music every Thursday night in The Village Forge in Concord's Colonial Inn for over forty years. He was born and raised in Concord. He spent ten years living in a small cabin close by the Concord River, in Carlisle, Massachusetts. He and his wife Denise have seven children, and now live "just up the river" near the Assabet in Maynard, Massachusetts. Fitz's published work consists of three books of poetry, a collection of essays, an anthology of original ballads, and his now classic album of songs, "Fires in the Belly."*

Facing the Empty Page

John "Fitzy" Fitzsimmons

"I, on my side, require of every writer, first or last, a simple and sincere account of his own life, and not merely what he has heard of other men's ..."
— Henry David Thoreau, *Walden*

I come to this empty page for wisdom and possibility. I imagine Thoreau did the same; and probably for the same reasons.
This page, barely edged by words, is a field yet tilled. I do not yet know who I am, for at any given time, I am a teacher or a poet, a songwriter or folksinger. By less equal turns, I am also an essayist, a woodcarver, a sailor, tinkerer, and curmudgeonly philosopher. It is a rare day that dawns for me without something worth doing or something that is asked to be done. The difficulty is doing what needs to be done. Each thing to its time. Each time it is due.

Today I am an essayist looking at this — an empty page into which I stir cud-like thoughts mixed with some unsettled sense of duty. The emptiness is a part of who I am — an unkempt time-filler looking for meaning. I am here doing the same thing I asked my freshman English class to do as weekend homework: go to a spot in nature and think — and then write. "Write from your heart and soul and mind and being, and yes, it is what Thoreau would do."

To practice what I preach, I do my assignment. My spot — my slice of nature — is a wet hillside field overlooking Cedar Lake in central Massachusetts. While it feels secluded, I hear the distant drone of the Mass Pike somewhere to the south of me. I am surrounded by songbirds — innumerable wrens and sparrows, a pair of cardinals, a nuthatch carrying a string of blue yarn, a solitary, extremely agitated blue jay, and some red-headed somethings I do not recognize — finches maybe, but I don't think so. I used to think I knew them all — birds at least, but not so much anymore. It is hard to carry everything into an older age. The flimsy canvas rucksacks of youth might have been better spent on heavy sea-chests — a bigger hold to store burgeoning memories and fleeting trinkets of experience — hard, palpable mementos I can hold in my hand.

What exactly does an empty page represent? A place to put what is written within you. The words are already there. You just need to tap the tree and pour words upon an empty page. Do not be discouraged. To search for sense is to baffle yourself. The first words are by necessity a scramble for meaning, an unclear image upon a distant horizon. Out of this scrambling screed exudes some elusive broth of truths. The more difficult task is to make sense of your sound — to make palpable what is, at first, ephemeral. That is the craft of a writer. Plank on plank. Nail beside nail. Art follows craft in any endeavor. We are not yet artists.

Mine is a willful search, and, as always, I am hampered by my limitations, trapped as I am in the corporeal body I dwell in. I have yet to push the limits of what I know into the murky world of unknowing. I trust some nugget of wisdom lies within. When I am at a total loss, I turn to my journal, poetry, and prayer; when I am searching, I turn to the essay; and when I am perplexed by the present, I sit and think. Then I walk. Every essay begins with a walk. That, too, I learned from Thoreau. Nothing is lost in the pondering, but everything is lost in giving up the search.

What can Thoreau possibly tell us today? Simple. Reading Thoreau's writing is an exercise and an exploration that can literally change your life, if in any way, shape, or form your life wants or needs changing. The harsh truth is, if we do not change, we do not grow; hence, we are destined to consign our lives to a desperate search for meaning within the confines of a common life — an "unexamined life," Thoreau argues, is not worth living.

Thoreau found, shaped, and nurtured wisdom out of the natural world around him — but so have, and so do, many other slavish writers and pondering poets. I am not amazed by Thoreau's thinking, nor am I enamored of his life. I am amazed how he crafted, out of tomes of journal writing, crystalline gems of words, phrases, sentences, and passages that continue to ring in the modern mind with unnerving clarity and persistence.

Thoreau is most remembered for a few of his essays, a few extended travelogs and his one enduring masterpiece, *Walden*. I would argue he deserves to be most remembered for his insistence to live the life of a writer, a naturalist, and a philosopher. He measured and cataloged the natural world around him; he read broadly and deeply; he captured in each day the physical world around him and the metaphysical world within him in a voluminous series of daily journal entries. He distilled the essence of his utterly common life into the uncommon beauty of his remembered words. It is a greatness worth imitating.

You might see no need to change; you may feel no need to grow beyond what you are and what you aspire to be. As teachers and parents, we fill you with expectations and admonitions. We rob you of childhood and strangle your adulthood. We coddle you and call it caring; we implore you to act and be a certain way. We are convinced we know a better path for you; we implore you to accept our wisdom and grow fruits in line with our expectations. More often than not, we are wrong. You know it, and I know it. Only you can do anything about it. You are the inimitable you. There is nothing and no one else in the universe exactly like you. Every word you place upon the page in an honest and sincere search for truth is as real as an acorn dropped from the towering oak of your life. Cover that husky seed in moldy soil — that pithy promise that is inevitably you.

Nurture your life and become who you are — who you really, really are.

This is what Thoreau would do. This is what he did.

Will you?

Adam Gamble *is the author of* In the Footsteps of Thoreau: 25 Historic & Nature Walks on Cape Cod. *He is publisher at Good Night Books and On Cape Publications. His Good Night Series of illustrated children's books includes more than 200 titles.*

What *Wouldn't* Henry Do?

Adam Gamble

My studies of Henry David Thoreau focus on his visits to, and his book about, Cape Cod. In that regard, were he alive today, I believe he would still explore "the bared and bended arm of Massachusetts." Thanks to the protection afforded by the Cape Cod National Seashore, the outer beach that Henry explored has not been overexploited beyond recognition; and its essential nature remains inspirational, a place where "a man can stand and place all America behind him."

The primary logistical change to his Cape journey, were it to take place now, would be that rather than riding a train and then a stagecoach to the Outer Cape to begin his walk, he would have to take a bus instead, because it is now the primary public conveyance available. The primary existential change to Henry's Cape Cod, however, is that deaths at sea are far less common today than in the 19th century, the result of myriad changes in maritime safety. As a result, Henry would probably muse more about the perils of sea-level rise from climate change and pollution than about shipwrecks. Nevertheless, he would undoubtedly discover and celebrate just as much wildness and humanity here to write a classic book about Cape Cod.

Even more interesting to me is what Henry would *not* do. As a university student, he'd no doubt go to great lengths to avoid the student debt that is so common nowadays. Certainly, he would not take advantage of credit cards or other easy credit that would limit his freedom by requiring his labor to pay them off. Likewise, he would avoid places like today's ubiquitous convenience stores, recognizing them as the rather inconvenient consumer traps they are. He would not frequent restaurants, coffee shops, big-box stores, malls, or other non-essential shops. He would not be an Amazon Prime member. He'd even abstain from my own favorite spending vice, the local independent bookstore, sticking instead with libraries as he did in his lifetime. Henry wouldn't participate in today's hyper-consumerism, just as he resisted the 19th century's pale version of it.

Henry would not post many, if any, photos or videos or comments on social media. He wouldn't Tweet, Snapchat, Tik-Tok or be Linked-In. Facebook? Doubtful. He would have no interest in Pinterest. He wouldn't follow commercial television nor watch a lot of video apps like Netflix, et cetera. He would spot them as the "time-sucks" they are.

While his righteous passions would remain as powerful as ever, Henry would not take significant leadership positions in political or social organizations, any more than he ever did. This is not to say that he would not support today's civil rights, environmental, or social justice causes, that he would not be aware of social media, follow current events, or that he would not own a computer, or even carry a so-called smart phone (although the latter would be permanently set on mute). He was no hermit or Luddite. He was, of course, an abolitionist, participated in the underground railroad, and wrote *Civil Disobedience* and *The Last Days of John Brown*.

For Henry to be Henry, he would continue to care about his fellow homo sapiens, the rest of the natural world, and right and wrong. Unfortunately, as I type this, he also would also be living through the global Covid-19 pandemic, including the millions of deaths and illnesses, shutdowns, and social shifts it has wrought. These experiences would only intensify Henry's wish "to live deliberately, to front only the essential facts of life."

He would understand more than ever that, in order to live a life that inspires books like this one, published some 205 years after his birth, he would have to not do exponentially more today than he did not do in his own time.

Ultimately, it was Henry's intentional nonparticipation in so many thoughtless, superficial, and non-deliberate activities that permitted him to study so deeply (both written materials and the world around him), to contemplate so profoundly, to live so well, and to write so compellingly.

Now to the big obvious question implied by this book: What am *I* going to do?

Robert Ganz *taught English for 59 years. First at Harvard, then at Yale, the University of Virginia, and George Washington University from which he retired at 86. He held a Mellon Postdoctoral Fellowship. In the last months of WWII, he served in combat with the Tenth Mountain Division in Italy. He was brought up in Cambridge, Massachusetts, and now lives in Chilmark on Martha's Vineyard. He is currently writing a study of Robert Frost's poetry. It pays special attention to the poet's use of Emerson, Thoreau, William James, and Henri Bergson.*

Thoreau In Search of Ever Wakeful Readers

Robert Ganz

"'Tis pity if the case require...
We speak the literal to inspire
The understanding of a friend,"
— Robert Frost, who pillaged Thoreau repeatedly for more
than 60 years

"A poem should be about all. If it isn't about all it is nothing."
— Robert Frost, notebooks

In *Walden*, Thoreau was not primarily a naturalist or reporter, but
a poet writing in prose.

When he saw something or did something, he was apt then
to turn his attention to something quite different and of larger
significance. For example, when he was planting and working
in his bean field, he resisted sinking into being a farmer, relying
mainly on the farmer's manuals that began to be published in
New England a few years earlier. After several weeks of work, he
found it was "no longer beans that I hoed nor I that hoed beans."
A self-transformation and -enlargement had occurred.

In the years since *Walden* was published, we've become acutely
aware of farmers with very constricted aims who, for example,
send chemical fertilizer down nearby streams; or poison the
weeds and other plants of their neighbors as well as their own; or
damage the aquifer; and kill the bees; or mistreat those they hire
to pick their crops; or, as in the 1920s, unknowingly turn large
swatches of prairies into dust bowls.

Thoreau had a greater sense of serving the general welfare. This included planting extra for the woodchucks who came into his fenceless field and helped themselves to the burgeoning crop.

In *Walden*, he was primarily concerned with widening the scope of his attention beyond the bounds of the merely practical and material.

Walden depicted the transformation of ordinary seeing into imaginative seeing.

In quoting the saying of Democritus that "truth lies at the bottom of a well," Thoreau was in effect enlarging the nearby well into something else, namely a symbol. The saying implies that truth is always bounded and shaped within the outline of one's own sensibility, which boundedness was represented by the well-curbs. Reality, then, was always insular or personal.

Thoreau then went on to joke that the original name for his pond was Walled-in Pond, that which would be scooped up by the hands of his mind to become symbolic of all bodies of water and many other things as well. With strokes of wit he repeatedly reminded us of this duality separating matters of fact and symbol.

Thus, he said that the well as symbol is more serviceable than the fact that it keeps butter cool. And later on, as he meticulously measured the bottom of the pond with a plumb line, he paused in this exercise in dogged empiricism to rejoice that he had found the pond to be deep enough to be a symbol.

He meditated on the meaning and nature of this transformative seeing. In effect he was climbing out of what he was thinking or doing in order to contemplate its significance. He told us, "I am often beside myself."

And his reader should do something similar and keep considering not just what is seen but *how* it is seen.

Emerson, upon whose land Thoreau built his hut, said, "What we are, that only can we see." Or let's say what we perceive depends on both who and *where* we are and *where* we have been.

Early on, Thoreau announced that "I went into the woods because I wished to live deliberately, to front only the essential facts of life, and see if I could not learn what it had to teach, and not, when I came to die, discover that I had not lived."

In the same chapter, he also urged, "Let us settle ourselves, and work and wedge our feet downward through the mud and slush of opinion, and prejudice, and tradition, and delusion, and appearance…"

Only twenty-seven years after Thoreau's early death, at 44 in 1862, when *Walden* was still relatively unknown and underappreciated, another accomplished poet of nature, John Burroughs, wrote in *Indoor Studies* (1889) that Thoreau's "… eye … was full of speculation; it was sophisticated with literature, sophisticated with Concord, sophisticated with himself. …His mood was subjective rather than objective. He was more intent on the natural history of his own thought than on that of any bird. … From his journal it would seem that he was a long time puzzled to distinguish the fox-colored sparrow from the tree… he was looking …intently for a bird behind a bird — for a mythology to shine through his ornithology."

Thoreau's overriding intention, to find the birds behind the birds, rightly diverted him from the task of merely identifying birds as in distinguishing the fox-colored sparrow from a tree.

He was looking for the more significant bird than the one in the field guides. Thoreau's bird is the one that can only be seen with the eyes of the speculative mind funded by a wide range of interests and previous experience.

Almost everything in *Walden's* landscape was seen or heard in perspective. The pond and surroundings seen from a small hill were changed by being reflected in the surface of the pond and the far shore seemed to disappear — it looked larger than it was. The view of the pond and its environs as seen from the hill transformed the landscape.

Thoreau said that the view he saw had become watery or fluid. Of course, the objective landscape in front of him hadn't changed at all.

But in going on to tell us that in comparison the land surrounding his hut "was but dry land" he was intimating that the "fluid" view from the hill was superior. Without his comment one might have dismissed the view as an optical illusion but the implication here is that it brought out something far more important than what it obscured. The more important fact was the amenability or tendency of things or objects, wherever they are, to be affected by the thrust of our imagination toward them.

In the conclusion to *Walden*, Thoreau praised the value of writing extravagantly — wandering outside the strictures that confine normal discursive prose in order to suggest one or more meanings that are difficult to state directly.

In *Walden* Thoreau's mind often grew downward, wedging further into nature and also into the self, to the consciousness that as Wordsworth said, "… lie too deep for tears." And one may suppose too deep for translation into words and instead into that place below "the mud and slush of opinion, and prejudice, and tradition, and delusion, and appearance…"

Perception at its best is discovery, not just confirmation of the given. The penultimate sentence in *Walden* runs as follows, "only that day dawns to which we are awake."

Patricia J. Núñez García *is a Sustainable International Development specialist and climate advocate. She is a volunteer of The Climate Reality Project and a member of its Boston Metro chapter. Patricia teaches climate change courses in universities in Spain (Universidad Libre Internacional de las Américas) and Chile (Pontificia Universidad Católica de Valparaiso). Her climate work with youth and professionals who are interested in solutions to adapt to and mitigate climate change continuously shape the way she communicates about this global challenge and its effects on "the tolerable planet" we all need and want.*

Observe, Resist, and Reflect

Patricia J. Nunez Garcia

I met Henry D. Thoreau in autumn 2013. His hand raised to chest height and the strength of his step spoke to me of conviction. Of course, I am referring to the statue outside his cabin's replica, where I stood again in the spring of 2021, asking: "Mr. Thoreau, as a climate advocate and a mother worried about my child's future in a planet with an unstable climate, how can I catalyze others and myself to effectively support climate action?" Henry, as he asked me to call him, responded: "Observe, Resist, and Reflect."

It was a warm day and I had brought Henry chilled Rhubarb Shrub.

Observe

"The question is not what you look at, but what you see."

First, understand the climate influencers and how far they've let their private feelings interfere with the public good. "Could a greater miracle take place than for us to look through each other's eyes for an instant?" Henry asks. I see him recalling failed attempts to make others see justice. Henry shares his eye-opening experience with the institution of jail where he "comprehended what his town's inhabitants were about."

Henry warns me that I "cannot expect, like Orpheus, to change the nature of the rocks and trees." I write down: "Know your enemies and allies, it might be the same person at different times. Know their priorities and connect them to climate action." Henry reads this, smiles, and says: "A fact stated barely is dry. It must be

the vehicle of some humanity in order to interest us. ... A man
has not seen a thing who has not felt it."

Occasionally, I think climate action has gained momentum as
a co-benefit of society's natural inclination toward survival and
progress, rather than as a stand-alone objective. Henry shrugs;
he's suspicious and warns, "action from principle, the perception
and the performance of right changes things in relations .... It not
only divides States and churches, it divides families; ay, it divides
the individual, separating the diabolical from the divine." I realize
it isn't simple or easy, but I'll pay the price, to an extent. Henry
notices that I feel lonely and, sometimes, muted. He understands
and says: "any (wo)man more right than his neighbors constitutes
a majority of one already. ... (Furthermore), if I could convince
myself that I have any right to be satisfied with men as they are,
and treat them accordingly, and not according, in some respects,
to my requisitions and expectations of what they and I ought to
be, then, ... I should endeavor to be satisfied with this as they
are."

Resist

Henry ponders and explains that he is not anti-government,
and supports expedient and better government. He believes the
machine of government needs friction to move, which comes
from resistance. He notes, "If we were left solely to the wordy wit
of legislators in Congress for our guidance, uncorrected by the
seasonable experience and the effectual complaints of the people,
America would not long retain her rank among the nations ... it
must have the sanction and consent of the governed." Therefore,
we should trust democracy, look for compromises, and build
consensus.

I understand trade-offs are necessary, but ... I stop. I hear a
crack in the statue. Henry has seen well-intended citizens be
unconscientious, and governments pitifully unjust. "I do not lend
myself to the wrong which I condemn!" He hopes I won't either.

A bird poops on Henry. I quickly clean off the white mess, though I know the rain later that day will wash it away. "That was a Whip-poor-will, it came early," says Henry, appreciating being cleaned. This distraction relaxes the conversation again.

Reflect

"This is hard."

Henry acknowledges the system makes it impossible to live honestly, comfortably, in outward respects. Nevertheless, he cannot spare reminding me that "the cost of a thing is the amount of what I will call life which is required to be exchanged for it, immediately or in the long run."

A raindrop alerts me it is time to go. I stand and leave the statue, but I take with me the essence of the man — a mentor and a friend. I am less lonely now.

Robert A. Gross *is the James L. and Shirley A. Draper Professor of Early American History Emeritus at the University of Connecticut. Focusing on the history of Concord, he is the author of* The Transcendentalists and Their World *(2021) and of* The Minutemen and Their World *(1976; 25th anniversary ed., 2001), winner of the 1977 Bancroft Prize.*

The Man of Concord

Robert Gross

At a time when the social bonds among Americans are thinning, when millions accept big lies about election fraud while denying any responsibility to protect themselves and their neighbors against a deadly virus, and millions of other Americans join in mass demonstrations for racial justice, does Henry Thoreau's politics of the individual still have relevance?

At first glance, the answer appears to be no. Thoreau eschewed the exercises of citizenship in the popular democracy of his day. He didn't vote, stopped signing petitions against slavery to state and federal governments, didn't participate in town meeting. He loathed political parties in an era of intense partisanship. In his view, "men are degraded when considered as members of a political organization." He put his trust in the 18th-century ideal of the disinterested statesman, who deliberated rationally and acted impartially for the public good, with no thought of gain to himself. He had absorbed that elitist outlook at Harvard and never shook it off. "Why does [the government] not cherish its wise minority?" he asked rhetorically. Thoreau deferred to individual judgment, not to majority will.

Fittingly, we hail Henry for his solitary protests. True to his word, he acted alone on moral principle, without consulting anyone else and with no concern for costs and consequences. He was faithful only to conscience. When the right thing needed to be done, "the man of Concord" would do it boldly, whether that was ringing the meetinghouse bell for an anti-slavery gathering, refusing to pay taxes for an immoral war on behalf of slavery, ferrying a fugitive slave to freedom, or defending the character of John Brown after Harpers Ferry. Nor did he hasten to explain himself. His "resistance to civil government" went unpublicized. By the time he published his manifesto, the war had been over for a year. Thoreau's protest would influence posterity, not contemporaries. In his mind, the act should speak for itself. The righteousness of a cause was embodied in the character of its supporters. Thoreau admired Wendell Phillips for his authenticity, "unconsciously" revealing his biography as he set forth his convictions. The man and the cause were one.

As much as we can admire Thoreau for refusing to be an instrument of injustice — a moral stance as indispensable today as in his time — his disdain for collective action is troubling. Rarely does he acknowledge his social context and cultural milieu. His hostility to slavery did not spring spontaneously from his "moral sentiment." The young man came of age in Concord's first family of abolitionists, absorbing the radical sentiments that led his parents and sisters to embrace William Lloyd Garrison's call for "No Union with Slaveholders." He clearly felt their influence, even as he charted his own way. Publicly, he declared independence; privately, he acknowledged the ties of interdependence. The bonds he prized were social, not political.

In his essay on civil disobedience, Thoreau portrayed his confrontation with "the tax-gatherer" as a moral test of both men. In everyday life the two were neighbors, regarding one another with mutual respect. But in his public role, the constable embodied the authority of the state. Thoreau denied that claim. Refusing to pay the poll tax — a prerequisite for voting — he seceded from government rather than participate in its immoral acts. Would the official recognize the delinquent "as a neighbor and well-disposed man"? Or would he take action against "a maniac and disturber of the peace"? Alas, the amiable neighbor dissolved into an unthinking agent of injustice.

This standard of neighborliness opens the way to an ethic of interdependence. Thoreau recognized that "to act collectively is according to the spirit of our institutions" and cheerfully paid taxes for libraries and schools. Cooperation with others was the essence of neighborliness, and so the Harvard graduate reached across the barriers of race and class to forge connections with ne'er-do-well Yankees, Irish immigrants, and Black laborers. "Could a greater miracle take place than for us to look through each other's eyes for an instant?" Thoreau asked and then added that "a miracle … is taking place every instant." On that struggle for mutual understanding our future depends.

Barbara Hanno *was fortunate to become a guide at the birthplace of Henry David Thoreau, her hero from childhood, after she retired in 2016. During her college years, she earned a Bachelor of Arts in English, with a concentration in the Transcendentalists. One of her delights is organizing personal historical and genealogical field trips for family and friends (like Henry). She is an avid photographer and also enjoys driving her Morgan mare, Lark, along the back roads of her small country town. She and her husband, Philip, and her family, live in central Massachusetts, not very far from Mount Wachusett and Mount Monadnock.*

Henry's Field Trip

Barbara Hanno

Just for this book, *What Would Henry Do?*, I asked Henry if he'd trade a field trip in our present world in exchange for any advice he might give us. "I will tour first," he bargained. "We'll see what the world brings!" We decided to meet at his birthplace, Thoreau Farm, in Concord.

Henry was waiting for me, sitting on the comfortable bench by the kitchen garden, when I arrived in the yard of the pristine white colonial house at Thoreau Farm. Vines of peas twined and bloomed along the garden fence.

"This is my birth house?" he immediately asked, puzzled. "This is not where I remember my mother dreamed on the doorstep, listening to the farmers whistling home."

"The house was moved to this spot from down the road a century or so ago," I said. "Come along and we'll look around."

"The house looks magnificent for its ancient age," said Henry. We sauntered under a shady oak tree. Henry picked up an acorn and tossed it at the second story window, pinging on the glass. "That's the room where I was born."

I explained to Henry that the Thoreau Farm Trust saved the house from demolition and completely restored it. The headquarters of the Thoreau Society now reside here. Furthermore, writers are invited into Henry's birth room, to write furiously, while the heat is in them, drawing inspiration from the spirit of the place.

Henry looked greatly pleased. We walked over to the solar panels behind the house and admired them. Beyond, we could see the fields of Gaining Ground, the farm based on the property, that grows food for the hungry.

"A perfect use for my old home," said Henry.

After leaving the farm to go to town, we walked through the center of Concord, where we stopped by a plaque that proclaimed this the spot where Henry had spent the night in jail. He refused to pay his poll tax, because the tax supported the Mexican War, which was perpetuating slavery.

"It was a powerful moment. It was an honor to spend the night in jail," Henry announced. "Standing up for what is true and right should be our clarion call."

We strolled past the Colonial Inn to The Old Manse, the home of Ralph Waldo Emerson's ancestors. We could hear bagpipe music and singers serenading through the trees.

"Shall I play my flute?" said Henry, pulling his flute out of his pocket. "I can follow the cadence with a lively melody."

"Oh, wonderful, but we should just listen. It is the outdoor walking play, 'Nature,' written and performed by a descendant of Waldo and Lidian. We should listen and follow."

We walked along the rim of the crowd, as the actors moved about the fields behind The Old Manse, dancing, singing, laughing, and recreating the lives of Waldo, Henry, and their friends.

"So movingly done," Henry sighed. "All these were my dear friends. But where is Ellen Sewall?" There is no remedy for love, but to love more.

As we had a long drive to make before sunset, we decided to move along. Henry approached my car with gingerly forbearance.

"Quieter than a train," he opined, with a slight frown and a look of reluctant curiosity, as we motored away.

We headed far westward, traversing hills and valleys and rivers, until we saw the hulk of the tallest mountain in Massachusetts, Mount Greylock, the great Saddle-back.

"This is, indeed, my temple," murmured Henry, as we parked the car at an access road to the Appalachian Trail. We hiked the rest of the afternoon, until we reached the summit. And while we reveled in the swirling mist, Henry revealed his advice.

"Preserve," he said. "Nature is full of genius, full of divinity. We must keep this earth green. The forests must grow, always cherished, and the water must always flow clear. In Wildness is the preservation of the world."

"Persist," he said. "Make your voice heard. Stand up against racism, hatred, greed. Follow the drumbeats of your truth. Find your deepest love and, always, be your innermost sacred Self."

We left Mt. Greylock and sailed home, eastward, toward the endless sunrise. "Only that day dawns to which we are awake... The sun is but a morning star."

Huey *(the pseudonym for* ***James Coleman****) has made 7 feature-length documentary films with his company, Films by Huey. He is a founder and director of the Maine Student Film and Video Festival, now in its 43rd year. He has been an artist-in-residence in animation and filmmaking in over 100 schools in New England. He is an adjunct instructor in Communications and New Media, Southern Maine Community College, South Portland, ME. In 2021, Huey was recognized by the Thoreau Society with The Walter Harding Distinguished Achievement Award in Scholarship.*

Lessons from *Surveyor of the Soul*

Huey

What Would Henry Do? was one of the reasons I made my film, *Henry David Thoreau: Surveyor of the Soul*. From the beginning of its thirteen-year production period, my goal for the film was to tell the story of Thoreau in his time and in ours. Early in the film, Robert Gross points out that Thoreau lived his life "implementing principle in action." I let my experiences as a filmmaker and educator and encounters with Henry guide me. Using that as a through-line, *Surveyor of the Soul* features many examples of people living their beliefs in the spirit of Thoreau's writings and lifestyle.

My first connection to Henry was an indirect one. When I was in high school a priest in my church gave a moving sermon about his experience in the Selma, Alabama, protest march over the Edmund Pettus Bridge on "Bloody Sunday." As we know, Reverend Martin Luther King, Jr. was a follower of Thoreau, as was John Lewis, the leader of the Selma march. The resonance of this sermon led me to ask Rep. John Lewis to be a part of *Surveyor of the Soul*. He graciously let me film him speaking in Boston, urging us to "march on."

After graduation from college, I became an educator, following a learning-by-doing approach to teaching that Henry practiced in his own private school. For example, I currently teach a course at Southern Maine Community College to help students understand how much media controls their lives. In "Introduction to Mass Communications," I assign a midterm for them to go 48 hours without media. I use Thoreau to provide the context for the assignment by assigning *Walden*, Chapter 2, "Where I Lived, and What I Lived For." I emphasize his quote:

"I went to the woods because I wished to live deliberately, to front only the essential facts of life, and see if I could not learn what it had to teach, and not, when I came to die, discover that I had not lived."

The concept of examining your life as if on your deathbed, and whether it was worth living, really grabs students' attention. They, like Henry, are at a time in their lives where they are grappling with essential questions.

In *Surveyor of the Soul*, the students of the Walden Project at Vergennes Union High School in Vermont can be seen in their "classroom" around a fire pit in the forest. Here with Walden Project founder Matt Schlein, students spend four days a week during the school year outdoors, guided by Thoreau's writings. We see them take on Thoreau's challenge to live deliberately in the midst of their classroom's natural environment.

In *Walden* Thoreau writes that he wanted "to brag as lustily as chanticleer in the morning, standing on his roost, if only to wake my neighbors up."

Despite this seemingly immodest statement, Henry was a follower of those who had lessons to impart. He did this through his association with the people in his community, notably Ralph Waldo Emerson and local farmers whose land he surveyed. This is exemplified in "The Succession of Forest Trees," a talk he gave as an invited speaker at the Middlesex County Agricultural Fair. It lays the groundwork for his ideas on what we now call ecology.

I was involved in the back to the land movement of the 1970s. Inspired by Helen and Scott Nearing, who in turn were inspired by Thoreau, young people took up farming in rural states like Maine. John Bunker, homesteader and longtime friend and associate from those years, is seen in the film harvesting wild apples and celebrating a Wassail like Thoreau writes about in his essay, "Wild Apples."

Joe Polis, Penobscot, was not only a guide for Thoreau on his third and final trip to the Maine woods, but also a great influence on Thoreau.

In my film, James E. Francis, Sr. and Darren Ranco, members of the Penobscot Nation, present their perspectives on Thoreau's encounters with their ancestors. Ranco, a descendent of Polis, explains how Thoreau's first trip was a missed opportunity because of his primitivism and false expectations of indigenous people. Yet by the third trip and after meeting Polis, Thoreau can be considered a progressive when it comes to his thinking about who Native Americans are and the role they play in understanding Nature.

In *The Maine Woods*, Thoreau writes that Polis told him, "It makes no difference to me where I am." Meaning he is equally at "home" in the woods as he is in his village. This was astounding to Thoreau, whose concept of Wildness was based on its separateness from Civilization.

In *Surveyor of the Soul*, Ron Hoag explains that Thoreau's trips to the Maine woods affected his thinking on nature, as in his essay "Walking," where he writes, "in Wildness is the preservation of the world."

Thoreau's lifestyle of living deliberately, his deep respect for nature, and his commitment to a community inclusive of all people were the ways he implemented principle in action. I believe what Henry would do is expect no less from us today.

Rochelle L. Johnson *currently serves as president of the Thoreau Society and is Chair of Environmental Studies at the College of Idaho. Her writing on 19th-century landscape aesthetics appears in a variety of journals and essay collections, and in* Passions for Nature: Nineteenth-Century America's Aesthetics of Alienation. *Rochelle has co-edited five additional books, including* Thoreau in an Age of Crisis: New Essays on an American Icon. *She is writing a book about Susan Fenimore Cooper (1813-1894) and environmental grief.*
Find more at: https://www.rochellejohnson.com

Surely, Anguish

Rochelle L. Johnson

One evening in the pandemic spring of 2020, a Cooper's hawk perched on my urban-backyard fence, yellow talons gripping pressure-treated picket. His small eyes, rimmed yellow, darted left, right, up into greening pear tree, down to white-blooming hostas. As daylight faded to the lilac grays of western sunset, his starkly mottled chest grew indistinct. He returned the next day and again the next, curved beak sharp, flashing fierce. In those moments, I felt such joy — just a little bit, just then, just there.

Each afternoon, I found myself hoping he would return yet again, though I felt guilty for hunting this pleasure. I knew that my gawking at what Thoreau labels "cheap summer glories" accomplished nothing, contributed nothing to solving the world's problems. Amid rising daily death tolls and heinous political leadership, when police officers took Black life after Black life, I should have been blind with anguish.

But I was not alone in seeing. Many noticed what they described as an extravagant spring. Like you, maybe, I read of people looking through window screens or from balconies, from patios or newly slung hammocks, claiming that maple leaves unfurled more elegantly, honeysuckles smelled extra pungent, white-breasted nuthatches peeped more emphatically than before. I know: this marveling was a privilege. And maybe denial. Or negligent frivolity. Still, it was as if, amid tens of thousands of extinguished heartbeats, those still beating suddenly felt what Thoreau called "the great pulse of nature."

Like us, Thoreau knew a deeply troubled and diminishing world. Nonetheless, in his first published natural-history essay, he wrote,

"Surely joy is the condition of life." It's shocking, really, that he made this audacious claim, and even more shocking that he routinely *felt* joy — which his capacious journal suggests he did, and regularly. He knew the pandemics of his own time: scarlet fever, cholera, and of course tuberculosis, which killed his sister and eventually him, too. Whereas we grieve persistent racism and police brutality, anthropogenic climate disruption, and stark political division, Thoreau grieved rampant "resource" extraction, a culture of busyness, private property, and land-grabs, and that his citizenship implicated him in the economics and viciousness of chattel slavery.

For us, as for Thoreau, surely anguish is the condition of life. But he wrote those joy-filled words anyway, apparently willing to set aside that, in the midst of devastation, delighting in a Cooper's hawk or publicly asserting one's experience of bliss can smack of temerity.

Sticklers may say that Thoreau published his declaration of life's joy in 1842, prior to some of the events I evoke above — before the Mexican-American War, for example, and before the Fugitive Slave Law. But these notable atrocities followed a deeply troubled past in the way that George Floyd's murder and an urgent planetary pause followed centuries of racial violence and ecological devastation. I could hardly be surprised that deadly tragedy grew out of our systemically racist past and destruction of global biodiversity, and I bet Thoreau was not entirely shocked at his nation's course. As Drew Lanham said mid-pandemic, "Our task . . . has been pathfinding through the improbable without ending up at the inevitable." We knew where we were headed as we inhabited this age of injustice and contagion; we just hoped we would not end up here.

What would Thoreau do when he glimpsed joy amid unfathomable anguish? I imagine: protest, petition, vote. Refuse allegiance, aid the innocent and the ill. Bow head into hands upon learning of yet another species in precipitous decline, still another mass shooting, more innocent pulses extinguished.

When Thoreau advises us to claim joy as what "vibrates through the universe," he also mentions "the inexpressible privacy of a life, — how silent and unambitious it is." So, I think he would do this, too: understand himself as like those who came before, those who likewise suffered silently through the improbable before arriving at the inevitable, grateful for mere survival. Like them, he would wait for the twilight possibility of a hawk's alighting and, if that gift arrived, greet mottled chest, yellow-rimmed eye, and gripped talons by clasping that wonder close, holding tightly, relishing one small moment that muted life's anguish — just a little bit, just then, just there.

Jennifer Johnson *is the Executive Director of Gaining Ground — a non-profit, no-till regenerative farm that donates 100% of what it grows to people experiencing food insecurity. Gaining Ground's fields are located behind Thoreau's birthplace. Jennifer is passionate about equitable access to healthy food and the healing power of nature. She's found her dream job at Gaining Ground and loves working with Gaining Ground's staff, board, volunteers, and partners to grow food and grow community. She lives with her family in Concord and enjoys reading, running, hiking, gardening, and kayaking.*

Agriculture Comes Full Circle

Jennifer Johnson

"The farmer increases the extent of habitable earth.
He makes soil. That is an honorable occupation."
— Henry David Thoreau, *Journal*, March 2, 1852

I don't think that the Henry of 1852 could have ever imagined that the "honorable occupation" of agriculture would end up accounting for more than 10% of greenhouse gas emissions in the U.S. in 2021. Or that too many farmers would destroy, rather than make soil.

A recent study published in the Proceedings of the National Academy of Sciences found the Midwestern section of the United States has lost more than 35% of its topsoil since plowing became mechanized. This topsoil loss then requires inputs of chemical fertilizers and pesticides in order to produce marketable crops. The chemicals make the land even less fertile (not to mention the damage done to the health of the people who farm the land and eat its crops!), which results in farmers having to use even *more* chemicals. And the downward cycle continues. In its quest for maximum productivity and economic gain, the modern farming system is making the land and people sick.

While Henry might certainly despair at the state of modern big agriculture, he'd no doubt champion the efforts of small farmers and the return of hand-scale agriculture.

Approximately 21% (and growing!) of U.S. cultivated farmland is managed using a system called no-till farming, essentially a return to the way humans have farmed for thousands of years prior to the invention of the mechanized plow. The goal of no-till farming is to minimize soil disturbance. Mechanized plows churn up the top 6 to 10 inches of soil between each planting. This leaves bare soil exposed to the elements (resulting in massive erosion) and destroys the trillions of bacterial, microbial, and fungal networks that nourish growing plants and keep soil healthy. In a no-till system, farmers eschew the plow in favor of broad forks and other hand tools that aerate the soil but keep it intact. Compost replaces chemicals and each successive crop adds more organic matter to the soil. No-till farmers focus on making soil, just as Henry wrote in his journal.

And what about those greenhouse emissions associated with agriculture? No-till farmers not only produce fewer emissions but can actually play a role in helping to draw down carbon from the atmosphere. Soil naturally holds the carbon that is captured by its growing plants. When left undisturbed, the soil will hold the carbon and prevent it from being turned into carbon dioxide. Scientists are still actively studying the role that healthy soils can play in sequestering carbon and reducing net greenhouse gasses, but the findings to date show that this is an area of great potential.

Across the country, more farmers are beginning to question the promises of "modern" agriculture and the relentless push for "efficiency." They are looking at their peers who have retired their rototillers, while at the same time improved their soil and harvests without turning to toxic chemicals. And they are beginning to wonder how they might join the movement. No doubt, Henry would approve.

Chynna Lemire *has been the Business Manager for The Thoreau Society for almost a decade. Having lived in New England her whole life, she finds her sense of place in Historical Concord and at Walden Pond. With undergraduate degrees in Literature and Philosophy from the University of Massachusetts Lowell, Ms. Lemire dedicates her time to preserving the ideas of the 19th century New England intellectuals with hopes that it will shape the quality of life for those of her generation.*

Divine Treasure

Chynna Lemire

Other than William Shakespeare, Henry David Thoreau is arguably one of the most quoted (and often misquoted) authors of all time.

"Advance confidently in the direction of your dreams!"

"Rise free from care before the dawn, and seek adventures."

I do not like rising before the dawn, and it is certainly never free from care. I will hit the snooze button for hours. However, if you enjoy observing nature like Thoreau did, you must grab your binoculars and get fixed on that fox den by dawn because that is when all the excitement happens.

Sleeping in is a wonderful thing, and self-care is a big topic for millennials these days. It is so much more than nice skincare products and the occasional bubble-bath. Self-care requires you to take a step back, reflect on your existence, and ask yourself, "what do I really need?"

What do you need? Food, water, sleep... and good mental health. What about the crippling existential dread you felt as you watched the Covid-19 numbers on your local news channel and how do you cope with all of the loss?

Thoreau can teach us all about self-care. While he was grieving the loss of his brother, he took the opportunity to spend some time alone. Two years, two months, and two days to be exact — but then he came home and shared with us what he learned. You will find quotes from Thoreau near the self-help section of your bookstore, or look for his books in sections on spirituality and mindfulness. *Walden* and the *Journal* are so comforting at times that some would consider it their Psalms.

We have been grieving through the pandemic for longer than Thoreau was living at Walden Pond. We have had to look loss right in its face. When I got furloughed in April of 2020, I sought out Thoreau's *Journal,* thinking I would get some comfort. At the time, it did not help. I thought, "maybe I picked the wrong volume to read." It was August of 1856 and I was knee deep in swamp water. Thoreau spent all day at the dismal bog collecting different kinds of cranberries and separating them into the pockets of his trousers. If not at the swamp, then he was on his boat the *Musketaquid*, paddling along the Assabet River to the same rock wall to note the water level. Or perhaps he would go for a morning walk, and almost always a walk in the evening. Then back to the cranberries and then again to the rock wall.

"Where is the philosophy in all of this? Is this Transcendentalism?" I wondered.

The pandemic forced a lot of us to spend time with only ourselves and our loss. I am a very social person and being alone was hard. Then my long-term partner left me out of the blue, and being alone became extremely hard. I started to realize that I had never actually hung out with just myself.

Some say that Ralph Waldo Emerson wrote about Transcendentalism while Henry David Thoreau practiced it. The whole idea behind transcending is intuitive. It is individualistic. It is totally romantic and poetic. In a way, it is self-care. You cannot have others there. Maybe you need to be alone in a bog. You will experience it, as William Wordsworth said in 1800, as "the spontaneous overflow of powerful feelings... recollected in tranquility." You will go home, change out of your swampy clothes, and, as you reflect, you may even start to write about your experience.

Transcendentalism is the act of being in the natural world alone, and it is there where you can let yourself experience the divine. You *will* find treasures there. You *must* stop and smell the

flowers. You could try to share the experience with someone —
your partner, your editor, your cat — but that little bit of divine
spark should be cared for and prioritized, and it is all for you and
your mental health. In 1847, when Thoreau returned home from
Walden Pond, he shared with the world what he could about his
experience. The rest of his divine treasures he got to keep for
himself.

Elise Lemire *is the author of* Battle Green Vietnam: The 1971 March on Concord, Lexington, and Boston, *as well as of* Black Walden: Slavery and Its Aftermath in Concord, Massachusetts, *and other titles. A native of Lincoln, Massachusetts, and a former member of the Thoreau Society Board of Directors, she is Professor of Literature, Purchase College, the State University of New York.*

What Henry Did in 1971

Elise Lemire

Posing the question of what Henry David Thoreau would do can have a powerful effect, as evidenced by an event that took place more than a hundred years after his death.

Members of Vietnam Veterans Against the War set out to march Paul Revere's mythic midnight route in reverse as a means of once again warning the people that an imperialist aggressor was invading the countryside.

The three-day march began without incident. The veterans had secured permission from the National Park Service to camp at Concord's Old North Bridge and to march eastward through Minute Man National Historical Park.

However, Lexington's Select Board had denied the veterans' request to camp on the Lexington Battle Green, and attempts by Lexington residents in the days leading up to the march to change the Board's mind had failed. And thus, after a dinner provided by Concord supporters at the Bridge, the veterans took a vote on whether to proceed onto the Green and thereby risk arrest.

"All those who are voting for civil disobedience in Lexington," intoned one of the march organizers, "raise your hand."

Four veterans voted against the measure.

"It seems to me that they could come in at four in the morning, when everybody else is asleep and the newsmen are in the sack and just round us up and cart us away," a veteran with black-rimmed glasses and a long dark beard worried. "No one will see it!"

Operating under majority rule, the veterans set aside this concern and prepared to march to Lexington the next morning.

Their first stop en route to Lexington was Concord's Monument Square. Running out from behind the clapboard and brick buildings that ring the expanse of grass located at one end of the town's store-lined Main Street, a large group of fatigue-clad men screamed "di di mao" (pidgin Vietnamese for "get down") at several of the people crossing the square. Brandishing very real-looking toy M-16s, the GIs forced their captives down onto the ground where, after only the briefest of interrogations, they summarily executed them. Other veterans distributed flyers assuring shocked bystanders that this was theater meant to prompt the public to ask what it must feel like to experience these kinds of atrocities every day.

The veterans carried out their mock search-and-destroy mission at this location because they knew there would be witnesses for their message that the public must rally to end the war. What they did not anticipate was the impact a small commemorative plaque to the side of the square would have on some of the participants.

Henry David Thoreau was imprisoned for one night in a jail on this site in July, 1846, for refusing to recognize the right of the state to collect taxes from him in support of slavery — an episode made famous in his essay "Civil Disobedience."

For a group of young people who wanted to end what they regarded as a gross injustice, this plaque had special resonance.

Later that day, when the bespectacled veteran with the long dark beard was interviewed on the Lexington Battle Green, he explained why he had changed his mind. He wanted to take a stand no matter whether anyone was there to see it or not.

"Thoreau went to jail for the same issues. There was a war on with Mexico in those days. The United States had invaded that country," he explained. "Thoreau wouldn't pay his tax. They put him in jail. You remember what Emerson said, don't you?"

He proceeded to describe Emerson's surprise at seeing his friend. "Henry! Henry! What are you doing in jail?"

In actuality, Emerson did not know that Henry was in jail until the next day, after Henry had already been released, but by 1971 the version of events told in Jerome Lawrence and Robert E. Lee's widely-performed new play, *The Night Thoreau Spent in Jail*, had trumped the facts.

"Waldo! What are you doing *out* of jail?" Henry replies in the play, chastising his friend for paying his taxes and thereby supporting an immoral government.

No one had mentioned Henry when the reluctant veteran argued against late night civil disobedience. Now, having passed the plaque in Monument Square marking where the Concord local was incarcerated, that same veteran was starting to listen to area residents linking the veterans' efforts to Henry's.

"This is the only chance in my life I'll have to imitate Thoreau and take this dare to be civilly disobedient," one local woman asserted of her decision to occupy the Green with the veterans.

"If dissent in of all places Lexington, right next to the birthplace of Thoreau, was going to be snuffed out, then everybody was going to suffer," was how another resident explained her decision to stay on the Green and possibly get arrested. "We would all lose our freedom."

And thus, after arriving on the Lexington Battle Green, where the veterans took a second vote to make sure that everyone was comfortable with the decision to occupy it without permission, the vote was unanimous. In the hours that followed, upwards of a thousand people sat down on Lexington's Green to assert their belief that the US must immediately end the war in Vietnam.

As some had anticipated, police did not arrive to arrest people until two in the morning. Nevertheless, the veterans and the hundreds of civilians who had decided to join them were all beaming when they were taken into custody.

Dissent was alive in Concord and Lexington once again, and asking what Henry would do had been the catalyst.

Because the mass arrest was the largest in Massachusetts history, the press did take notice. Pictures and stories ran on the front pages of newspapers around the country.

This and other actions taken by Vietnam Veterans Against the War ensured that President Nixon was unable to escalate the Vietnam War, which ended with Vietnam's victory four years later.

Michael Lorence *is president of The Innermost House Foundation, a nonprofit organization of volunteers dedicated to realizing the promise of a living transcendentalism to present and future generations.*

Beginnings

Michael Lorence

"Every morning was a cheerful invitation to make my life of equal simplicity, and I may say innocence, with Nature herself. ... I got up early and bathed in the pond; that was a religious exercise, and one of the best things which I did. They say that characters were engraven on the bathing tub of king Tching-thang to this effect: 'Renew thyself completely each day; do it again, and again, and forever again.' I can understand that. Morning brings back the heroic ages."
— Henry David Thoreau, *Walden*

Early in the spring of 1845, Henry Thoreau went to the woods in search of beginnings. The world about him was exploding with improvements, or with would-be improvements. Henry went to the woods to challenge the world. "Not till we have lost the world, do we begin to find ourselves, and realize where we are and the infinite extent of our relations." He went to Walden to lay the foundations for higher laws.

What were beginnings for Henry? Spring was a beginning. Morning was a beginning. The pond was a beginning. The woods were a beginning. Indian arrowheads were a beginning. The hearth fire was a beginning. Hounds, horses, and doves were a beginning. Homer was a beginning. The Bhagavad Gita was a beginning. Wildness was a beginning.

Henry's house began as a beginning, a primitive hall poised in a dream between heaven and earth, supported by strong-limbed king and queen posts, as of old. Its unfinished walls stood open to the elements and served as entryway to an adopted world of woodland creatures. It was a half-wild house, reclaimed from an archaic age and driven by changing times into a corner and reduced to its lowest terms.

If at length the house was plastered and enclosed, it was only to gather its three chairs of solitude, friendship, and society round an open fire against the coming winter. By the hearth, Henry kept his nights and entertained his guests. There he cooked his food and warmed himself and revisited human beginnings. There he conjured the first of companions. "You can always see a face in the fire."

By the winter of 1846, Henry's beginnings began to give way to an outward trajectory. At the edge of the following autumn, he left the pond forever. Henceforth the world that Henry knew would move forward, progressively approaching "no longer a poetic, but merely a chemic process." Whether he would or not, he had other lives to live.

What would Henry do today? Would he go again in search of beginnings as a foundation for higher laws? He would be older now. This is not spring but autumn. The hour of dawn is longer past. It is an unproven hypothesis that higher laws can be supported without foundations. For what were the higher laws he sought but a ripened innocence?

"But why I changed? why I left the woods? I do not think that I can tell. I have often wished myself back."

I think Henry recognized that his house was born to grow and decline and fall away. But in the late autumn of nature, as the world gives way evermore to would-be improvements, perhaps he would at last allow himself a way back. The Walden waters. The Indian arrowheads beneath his feet. The unnamed woods of our first home. In beginnings are the preservation of the world.

Carolina Maciel *is an undergraduate student from Rio de Janeiro. She's loves to cook, read, write, and hike. Her life changed when she read* Walden *at 22, dropping an almost-completed undergrad thesis on the Germanic educational system to start writing about New England Transcendentalism.*

Between the Woodland and Jail

Carolina Maciel

During the current pandemic, Thoreau's fame or Search Engine Optimization (SEO) continues to rise. All one has to do is Google "Thoreau," "pandemic," and "quarantine" to see how relevant Thoreau and his writing are today. While scholars have been working diligently to show the world that Thoreau was not a misanthropic hermit, nor a rebel for the mere sake of it, he is still mistakenly portrayed by many in the media — and therefore widely misunderstood — as only these two things.

In my reading of Portuguese, German, and Spanish language newspapers, many of the articles portray Thoreau as a lonely man dwelling between the woodland and the jail: nothing in between, nothing beyond. The frequent association between quarantine and *Walden* appears to carry two distinct meanings:

1. An idea that better understanding your own human capabilities and limitations helps you better examine your relationship with society, nature, technology, and consumption.

2. A vague analogy between the time Henry spent at his Walden house and being quarantined.

The first seems to have the power of bringing people closer to *Walden* or Henry's other works, as it makes Henry somewhat relatable and significant in our current times. I can suppose that Henry would appreciate the fact that there are people of all ages in various corners of the Earth eager to read his writings, considering how hard he worked.

The second, however, appears to be based on a poor reading of *Walden*, at best. Anyone who has read *Walden* is able to attest that if Henry's retreat was equivalent to our quarantine, then he would certainly have gotten sick and infected others. Thus, it is easy to imagine Henry cringing at people writing about *Walden* as if they had read it, when it's clear they had not.

Nevertheless, newspapers and magazine articles misreading *Walden* are relatively harmless and often historically inaccurate. Our bigger concern lies in the misreading of Henry's political ideas and the fact that there is an actual movement of people defining the act of not caring about the safety of others as an act of "civil disobedience."

There are dozens of videos on Youtube Brazil of people blasting denials of the pandemic itself, of vaccines, of death rates, and of the importance of wearing a mask as prophylaxis. They claim that one should go outside without a mask and there should be no restrictions at all, generally speaking.

There is even a Facebook filter with the following motto (roughly translated from Portuguese): "Get out of home! Civil disobedience calls us." Disrespectfully ironic, when we recall that Henry died from a lung disease.

Resistance to Civil Government tells us about an individual's relation to the State, indeed, but the principle behind such resistance should be ruled by morality and not shallow, whiny, egoistical refusal of both science and a basic sense of empathy.

When Henry resisted the government, he was selfless. He was not defending a warped concept of freedom. Would he accept all atrocities individuals and nations have inflicted in the name of freedom? I don't think he would ever consider it justifiable.

I would rather spare him from witnessing it all, especially since he would eventually find out that the people misusing his idea are the same people defending, in one way or another, child labor, 16-hour work shifts, logging, and poaching.

If Henry would say anything at all, I imagine he would say that true resistance should manifest through opposing a government that treats its citizens as modern-day enslaved people whose lives are literally disposable. Henry believed in everyone living a meaningful and joyful life, after all.

David Maguire, *author of* Here I Am: Concord Connections, *was raised in historic Concord, Massachusetts. His parents were told by his doctors that he would likely never walk, talk, or attend regular schools. Yet David's indomitable spirit resulted in such miracles as graduating from Concord-Carlisle High School and earning a B.A. in Education, Music and Humanities from Lasell College.*

How Henry is Alive and Well in Concord Today

David Maguire

"I have never gotten over my surprise that I should have been born into the most estimable place in all the world, and in the very nick of time, too."
— Henry David Thoreau, *Journal*, December 5, 1856

What did Henry mean? Henry had an interesting way of being proud and disappointed at the same time. I think he's saying America is a great country, yet he was born in the nick of time to do his part in making the country even better. He was very upset about issues related to government, social injustices, and the impact of population and industry growth. He even was willing to go to jail because he did not want to pay his poll tax to fund the government's war with Mexico, which would bolster slavery.

Henry wrote *Civil Disobedience*, which many think defines democracy in America. Henry argues people should not let government force them to do something that they think is wrong. Citizens have a duty to keep government from doing harm.

Henry loved Concord!

"Concord is my Rome," Henry asserted at a time when students took a grand tour of Europe immediately following their graduation from college. Henry stayed in Concord after graduating from Harvard, since he felt there was much to see and experience right at home.

I grew up in the same town as Henry and my home is on land
he surveyed. There are woods across the street from my house
and I like to imagine I am following the same paths he explored.
When I walk in these woods, I remember how he talked about
the importance of walks to think and relax. I don't believe it is
a coincidence that Concord today has so many beautiful places
to stroll and enjoy nature. In our small town, we have the
Concord Conservation Land Trust, the federal government's Great
Meadows National Wildlife Refuge, and Walden Pond.

Don Henley, of the band the Eagles, was inspired by Henry's
famous book, *Walden*. Even though he lived far away in Texas at
the time, Henley decided to invest in bringing more attention to
Henry's love of nature and founded the Walden Woods Project.

Anyone who visits Concord should experience how Henry is
honored in the Hapgood-Wright Forest, thanks to the Walden
Woods Project. As you walk along its paths, you will find quotes
from Henry etched in granite on the ground. It is as if he is
speaking to you along your walk. The big surprise is when you
reach the Reflection Circle. My father likes to call it Stonehenge.
In honor of Henry, some of the great minds in the world pay
tribute to him on the stones. Quotes are carved in stone from
famous people such as Ralph Waldo Emerson, Emily Dickinson,
Gandhi, Chief Standing Bear, Martin Luther King, and JFK. This is
a place to sit and relax after the uphill hikes.

Henry's passion for speaking out about social issues is still
evident in Concord, too. He fought against slavery, not only by
refusing to pay his poll taxes, but also by writing essays. Two
famous ones are, "Slavery in Massachusetts" (yes, we did have
enslaved people in Massachusetts) and "A Plea for Captain John
Brown." Today, you can find many "Black Lives Matter" signs
around town and you can often see people protesting war by
marching peacefully around our town center flagpole. These are
just examples of how Henry's beliefs in equality, social justice,
and peace live on.

Henry's last words were, "Moose. Indian." Once again, we need to ask, what did he mean? Was he expressing his lifelong love of nature? Or his ongoing concern about the mistreatment of people who are different? We all can wonder what was on his mind in his final hours.

James Marcus *is the author of* Amazonia: Five Years at the Epicenter of the Dot-Com Juggernaut *and seven translations from the Italian, including Giacomo Casanova's* The Duel. *He is the former editor of* Harper's Magazine *and has contributed to* The New Yorker, The Atlantic, The American Scholar, VQR, The Guardian, The Nation, *and* Best American Essays. *He also edited and introduced* Second Read: Writers Look Back at Classic Works of Reportage *and is currently at work on his next book,* Glad to the Brink of Fear: A Portrait of Emerson in Fifteen Installments.

Thoreau on Hold

James Marcus

Henry David Thoreau lived long enough to encounter the telegraph. Typically, he viewed this new technology with mixed feelings. It would be a conduit for so many wasted words — and yet a portal to the sublime!

"As I went under the new telegraph wire," he wrote in his journal in 1851, "I heard it vibrating like a harp high overhead." It was, he continued, the "sound of a far-off glorious life."

What he did *not* encounter, however, was the telephone, first patented nearly two decades after his death. Still less did he have any inkling of the telephonic limbo known as customer service.

What would Henry do if he were put on hold?

It's not hard to imagine. I see Henry weighing the smartphone in his hand and hesitantly dialing the number. There is a moment of silence. Then a human voice comes on the line: "Thank you for calling Bed, Bath, and Beyond, where we help you home happier!" This is a confusing sentence, an opaque sentence, dreamed up by a branding executive. It tramples on the English language — you can almost see the parts of speech quivering.

Henry, a great champion of verbs and nouns, would be offended. Yet he would stay on the line, because he needs supplies for his little shack out at Walden Pond. He waits, he listens to what he once called (in another context) the "unfinished silence" of the call. "How can I help?" the speaker resumes. By now the artificiality of the voice — its machine-tooled lack of human warmth — has made Henry uneasy, but he plunges on.

"I need two casks of lime," he says.

This ran him $2.40 back in the olden days, and he's prepared to pay a bit more. Yet the speaker says nothing.

"Are you there?" Henry asks.

"Using a few words, tell me how I can help you today," the voice pipes up.

"There's the lime," he responds. "And some hinges and screws. I paid about fifteen cents last time around."

There is no answer, no Muzak, no hiss on the line, not even a distant door slamming or the background badinage of birds. The phone is growing hot in Henry's hand. He is used to the emptiness of the natural world, which is not empty at all, but overflowing with perceptual riches. This is something else — an antiseptic parody of conversation, which is not always Henry's oyster to begin with, given his allergic reaction to small talk.

"You can ask for help with anything," the speaker says.

The phrase is a mild provocation for Henry. He has trained himself to ask for help with nothing, or close to it.

"The man who goes alone can start today," he wrote in *Walden*, "but he who travels with another must wait till that other is ready."

And yet perhaps his vaunted independence has been oversold, along with his vaunted solitude. A hermit in desperate need of other people, he entertained up to thirty guests during his watermelon parties at Walden, and even his little cabin required two or three friends to raise the frame.

But now the ghostly speaker continues: "Here are some examples."

She launches into a list of things, and many of them — like *consumer electronics* — seem like bits from an Orphic poem, random words whose destiny is somewhere far down the road, along with the hound, the bay horse, and the turtle dove that Henry claimed to have lost. The silence returns. Perhaps Henry has accidentally hung up the phone, having grazed with a knuckle that bright red circle that reminds him of the red elderberry, which "glows like the eyes of imps." The device is a kind of imp itself, is it not?

He regrets the call, but only a little. Surely this was the right number to dial. Bed (the frame of an old Chinese sofa) and bath (in the waters of Walden Pond, which impart to his naked body "an alabaster whiteness") are matters of ongoing interest. They are the stuff of life, the raw material of the senses. As for what is beyond — who would not wait forever, spending an eternity on hold, to get to the truth of that?

Author-Arctic explorer **Lawrence Millman** *has written 18 books, including such titles as* Our Like Will Not Be There Again, Last Places, Hiking to Siberia, At the End of the World, Fascinating Fungi of New England, Fungipedia, *and* Goodbye, Ice. *He has visited Henry's grave more times than he's visited either his mother's or his father's graves. He lives in Cambridge.*

Conversing with Henry

Lawrence Millman

For better or worse, Henry has become such a popular tourist icon that visitors to sites in Concord associated with him resemble moths flocking around a light. It's hard to guess whether Henry would have appreciated these acolytes, especially those brandishing Transcendentalist souvenirs.

On the one hand, he was a writer, and if there's anything a writer likes, it's attention. On the other hand, he probably would have run for the hills if these so-called acolytes started taking selfies with him. Or at least sauntered for the hills.

It's much easier to imagine his response to the environmental issues of the 21st century; issues so dramatically different from the ones in his own time that he might think he'd been transported not so much to another era as to another planet.

Contemplating the Sixth Extinction, atmospheric pollution, and runaway industrial development, he might phone (texting wouldn't be his thing) Emerson and say, "Ralph Waldo, I need a drink really bad. Please meet me at the Colonial Inn as soon as possible."

Over this drink, he might remark to Emerson, "It's a pity that a certain haughty primate hasn't joined all those other Sixth Extinction species…"

Let's now consider a particular environmental issue — the likelihood that plastics will outweigh all the fish in the world's oceans by the year 2050. Would Henry lead a protest march down the streets of Concord waving a banner that says, "Down

With Your Bloody Plastics!" Probably not, because he wasn't
a leader. Nor was he a follower. He was simply himself. But I
can imagine him holding a memorial service for the plasticated
oceans, as he did for John Brown, in the Concord Town Hall.

Upon his death, Henry believed he would become part of
the natural world rather than ascend to some sort of Celestial
Kingdom.

"Pine and birch, or, perchance, weeds and brambles will
constitute my second growth," he wrote.

In Concord's Sleepy Hollow Cemetery, I asked a white pine,
a yellow birch, a dandelion, and several prickly shrubs of the
rose family for their thoughts about climate change. There was
no response, so I asked these putative Henrys a more personal
question: "Aren't you afraid that you'll soon end up being
replaced by tropical vegetation, thanks to all this damn warming?"
Still no response.

I approached Henry's grave, a place where I hoped I might get
more intimate with the great naturalist than I'd gotten with his
botanical reincarnations. More intimate with him? Might I be
a psychic, a medium, or perhaps a necrophile? Not at all. It's
just that I think of Henry as being considerably more alive than
a goodly percentage of my living contemporaries, especially
those who've drowned themselves in the swirling jacuzzis of
algorithms. Thus, he might, just might, be capable of providing
me with some personal insights on the present state of the planet.

I was now standing at the grave, which had the usual votive
offerings — pebbles, shells, coins, and — of course — a rich
array of pencils. There was also a somewhat desiccated pickle,
perhaps placed at the grave by someone who wanted to tell
Henry that we're really in a pickle.

"What are your thoughts about these misbegotten times, Henry?" I
said to the grave.

As with the botanical specimens, there was silence, so I asked what I thought might be a more readily answerable question:

"Given the state of things now, would you be inclined to retreat to an unsullied place like interior Labrador or the Chesuncook area in Maine where you once went with Joe Polis? After all, Walden Pond and the Cape are so overwhelmed by recreational visitors that you wouldn't go to either place now in order to (as you put it in *Walden*) 'escape the noise of my contemporaries.'"

Again, there was silence, but then all at once I heard a white-throated sparrow in a nearby tree singing, "Poor Sam Peabody, Poor Sam Peabody," perhaps the saddest of all bird songs.

Might Henry have been using this sparrow as his mouthpiece in order to give me his thoughts on the current state of the planet?

John Hanson Mitchell *is the author of* Legends of the Common Stream, *the seventh in a series of books known as* The Scratch Flat Chronicles, *which explore the cultural and natural history of a single square mile of land northwest of Boston.*

Robin Hood and Henry Thoreau

John Hanson Mitchell

Some years ago, I started a book about the rise of private property and the loss of common land, told via the stories of two disparate characters, Robin Hood and Henry Thoreau. Just as I was starting the book, I became involved in an incident that dealt with the same issue, only in my case, the conflict involved not land, but a canoe.

Not far downstream from what is now Mass Audubon's Brewster's Woods on the Concord River, there was an abandoned boat house, with three or four unused canoes lying around the building, overgrown with bittersweet and brambles.

In those years, I was on the hunt for a small, single-person, second-hand canoe, not a common item in the used boat world, and there, among the full-sized canoes, I found one. It had lain exposed to rain for so long that a mat of duckweed was growing on the waters inside the hull.

I used to walk that river trail over a period of years and all that time, the boat lay there, slowly returning to earth. At one point I heard that the property had been sold to a very rich man who had torn down the former house and built a mansion high on the hill above the river. Good, I thought, surely this new owner will rebuild the boathouse and salvage the old canoes. But no, the years passed, and the boathouse lay in ruins, with its surround of canoes.

Given this situation, a friend of mine, a Robin Hood sort of fellow, said I should just take the canoe. No one would even know. The real Robin Hood would, of course, agree. No harm in stealing from the rich to supply an impoverished writer with a cast-off boat.

But what would Henry say?

We know he believed that a man is rich in proportion to the number of things he can afford to let alone. On the other hand, he did own a boat (although he complained about the fact that he had to pay taxes on it). He also pointed out that money is not a necessary element of one's soul.

I grew up messing about in boats; they are part of my soul, so, according to Henry, I shouldn't have to pay anyone for the canoe. Furthermore, like his compatriot, Robin Hood, Henry had a little problem with the rich.

"The more money, the less virtue," he wrote.

Also this: "Lay not up for yourselves treasures upon earth where moths and rust doth corrupt and thieves will break in and steal:"

If I, the thief, steal the boat, am I not just playing an existential role? The canoe in its current state is doomed. And anyway, when the tax collector comes around, the rich owner will not have to pay taxes on the canoe if I take it, so I am saving him money — not that he needed any more.

Given these opinions, it would seem that Henry would approve of the fact that I liberated the canoe and put it to good use, exploring the same waters that Henry himself enjoyed. Anyway, everyone has a devil in him that is capable of any crime, he believed.

According to federal law, it is of course illegal for me to steal the canoe. But then Henry's views of government are notoriously libertarian. It is possible that, in this case, I, an individual, may be right and the government and its laws wrong.

Robin Hood would agree, of course.

But I am closely associated with a sort of virtuous Maid Marian who believes that it is not only illegal for me to liberate the canoe, but also, laws notwithstanding, unethical. She claimed I should contact the owner and ask to buy the canoe, which, in the end, I did.

Ironically the owner turned out to be a generous sort and charged me all of twenty-five dollars, which, Maid Marian claimed, he did in order to save face for an impecunious water rat such as myself.

Dr. Barbara Mossberg *is an educator with a career spanning more than 50 years. She has served as president of Goddard College, founder and president of the Emily Dickinson International Society, Laureate/Poet in Residence Pacific Grove, California, and creator and host,* The Poetry Slow Down.

Mossberg's book on Emily Dickinson, When A Writer Is A Daughter, *was Choice Outstanding Academic Book of the Year. Her lectures, worldwide in over 26 countries, feature Thoreau, including for the Thoreau Society at Jyvaskyla University, Sweden. She is Professor of Practice at the Clark Honors College at the University of Oregon.*

Perturbing Despair:
A Double Portrait of Thoreau as Chanticleer and Bug

Barbara Mossberg

The question *WWHD?* says it all. Yes, says, not asks.

According to linguist Suzanne Langer in *Philosophy in a New Key*, a question declares something known. The statement is "Henry would do . . . ." Knowing what he did, we imaginatively engage with this question. Wouldn't Thoreau be so at home in our times, urging fellow citizens to action — addressing a rally, hosting a podcast, narrating a PBS special as he rows on the Concord, leading virtual nature walks, tweeting @chanticleer @morning, speaking to crowds for BLM and climate change, fundraising a U.S. walkathon to Oregon #IwillwalktoOregon, making a virtual Nobel Peace Prize acceptance speech (no new clothes)?

A prototype action hero, he used words on both literal and poetic feet, sauntering the talk of social conscience. He demonstrated words as powerful action, actionable. Opposed to the Mexican American War for its intent to sustain U.S. slavery, he was not opposed to conflict and opposition: he championed John Brown's armed insurgency, and made public his protests of immoral law or war. He voted with his feet, to Walden, to jail, to political advocacy, for causes then considered eccentric and quixotic if not doomed. On the right side of history, he seems to have lived for our times, not his.

For years, there were two Thoreaus transforming our society. One was at the heart of the environmental preservation movement:

his words "in Wildness is the preservation of the earth" were
an anthem of the Sierra Club and other environmental groups.
Another was the "civil disobedience Thoreau" who influenced
M.L. King, Jr., Gandhi, and Tolstoy and our own days' civil and
environmental rights movements. HD was taught in separate
departments — political science, natural science, and humanities.
There seemed different, parallel tracks for expressing conscience
in our society.

But if we look at Thoreau's life and writing as one piece, as
we must do if we are asking, *What Would Henry Do?*, we see
advocacy of human freedoms and nature as one. In times like
ours, a fraught, jostled awakening to mandates and challenges to
teach how lives and wildlife and glaciers and permafrost matter,
Thoreau is an influencer with millions of followers who shows us
that seeing justice as essential for each of us and Earth can unite
us across demographics of age, culture, politics, gender, religion.
Such a vision is a role model for activism, not only as a writer
and speaker, but educator. For lifelong learning (a pleasure),
he would teach a different pedagogy and curriculum, an anti-
method epistemology, a taxonomy of rights based on his own
drumbeat of conscience for lifelong learning about the world.
Promising he would "learn from Indians" and the huckleberry
patch, he provides guidance on a new academics, how to be
wisely inclusive as we contend with climate change and a history
of social inequity.

Would teach? HD would say *what do you mean? I am teaching!
Here you are, learning from me* — and so we are. Yes, our
problems in our world today are enormous. But as Jonathan
Schell in *Fate of the Earth* argues, without hope we cannot
imagine and fight for solutions. What Thoreau did, and does,
is bug us and disrupt us out of apathy and despair. He begins
Walden as Chanticleer, waking us up; he concludes with the
parable of the bug egg alive, still, yet, after all, out of darkest
moments, from the unlikely tree plank cut long ago, emergent
hope, indomitable life, resurrection. There is more day to dawn.

Thoreau leads us with the ingredient our environmental and social movements need beyond love and outrage.

With hashtag @morning, @chanticleer he would tweet, write editorials, anchor talk shows, and march, using social media to deliver corny advice our world needs now: warnings and hope. He would use his immortal voice. WWHD? He already has done — and caused. As an influencer, he inspires us to ensure many mornings to come. As we ponder WWHD, knowing how his words and actions "egg us on" and matter, when he seemed a disregarded nobody in his day, we can *do*, too: we can believe that what we do for Earth and justice matters, no matter how it seems to the bug from inside the wood.

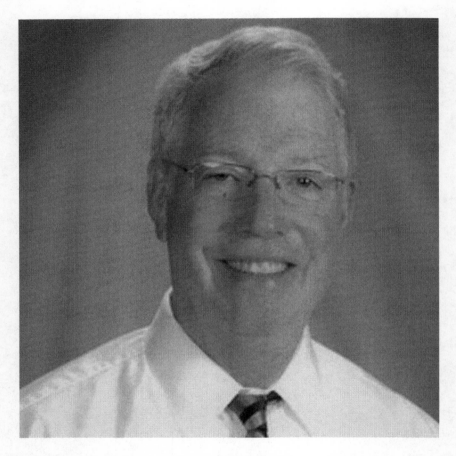

Tom O'Malley *teaches in the English department at Canisius College. He was awarded an NEH Fellowship in 1984 to study the Concord writers with Dr. Walter Harding in Massachusetts. His publication credits include short stories and essays for the* English Journal, The Christian Science Monitor, The Buffalo News, The Concord Magazine, *and various literary magazines and anthologies. Tom and his wife, Meg, are proud parents of three children and nine grandchildren.*

Writing with Henry

Tom O'Malley

Every teacher needs a mentor. For modern educators, it's a necessity. What with all the theories, strategies, lesson plans, faculty meetings, and student advocacy groups, one needs to find a partner who knows how to keep his or her feet on the ground. Over the years, I've never found a better schoolyard companion than Henry David Thoreau. I know he died in 1862, yet, luckily he left his voice with us in the form of two wonderful books and his grand opus, the *Journals*.

Thoreau's journals were not published during his lifetime, and I suspect he might not appreciate the fact they are readily available even today. Henry was a precise writer, fond of editing and revising his work — honing it to literary sharpness. Perhaps that is why his voice still speaks to us here in the 21st century. My life in the classroom is often a combination of problem solving, hand-wringing, shoulder-leaning and all sorts of listening opportunities. Henry has been my mentor and guide through all the challenges of working with young learners who can feel bored at times.

In his journal for June 27, 1840, Henry also dealt with boredom: "I am living this 27th of June, 1840, a dull cloudy day and no sun shining." I never realized life could be dull in the 19th century, what with all the discovering and Civil Warring going on. Yet there it is. This is the kind of day the history books ignore. Students often suggest that this is a world without computers, or streaming movies. What can you expect but boredom? Still, not one to give in, Henry found that boredom could be a useful part of life. He did this by taking up journal writing in a serious way. I like people who turn a perceived bad into a perceptive good, and that's what he did. Notice the good, careful observation on that 27th of June entry. It's just an ordinary day, but Henry turned it into something special by paying careful attention and then writing about it. There's a lesson in all this for my students and their teachers.

Journal writing went on at an almost daily pace for Henry, and it does for my students as well. Oftentimes, writers sit and hope for those moments of inspiration. I can see my students waiting for the muse to descend and inspire them. Henry also dealt with this on January 29, 1851, when he wrote: "Of all the strange and unaccountable things, this journaling is the strangest." See what I mean? There's no waiting around for writing or most kinds of learning. Henry got the journal-writing bug from his mentor, Ralph Waldo Emerson, who asked Thoreau: "What are you doing now?" That simple statement inspired him to explore the question for the rest of his life.

In *Walden*, Henry wrote: "The mass of men lead lives of quiet desperation." My students talk often of desperation, too — the desperate need to get their grades up, the desperate need for someone to notice them, the desperate need for teachers to listen to them. Later, Henry proclaimed: "I went to the woods to live deliberately." If the mass of men and women are quietly desperate, perhaps the answer is to live deliberately. Both Henry and I found that writing is the way to live deliberately. When we write in the journal we take time to really think things through and make meaningful connections.

As they grow and prepare for the new world beyond school, our students will be required to begin living deliberately. Notice the word "liberate" hanging around in that word so coyly. Thoreau found this to be the remedy for the desperations of his day. It is the way to the good life and real freedom after all. These young people in my classes will be working in fields that don't even exist right now. Many of them say they want to change the world. I take them seriously and respect their desire for change. How to prepare for that kind of a future? Pick up a pen and write, with Henry.

Sarah Oktay is currently the Director for Strategic Engagement and the Director of Stebbins Cold Canyon for the University of California Davis' Natural Reserve System. She received her B.S. in Marine Science and a Ph.D. in Chemical Oceanography from Texas A&M University-Galveston. From 2003-2016 she was the Executive Director of the University of Massachusetts-Boston Nantucket Field Station. She is the Past President of the Society of Women Geographers. She served as President of the Organization of Biological Field Stations, a professional organization representing several hundred field stations across the globe, from 2014-2016, and has been on the board for twelve years. She was the science advisor for actor and activist Mark Ruffalo for three years, advising on science topics for his environmental non-profits.

Finding the Next Henry

Sarah Oktay, Ph.D.

"Spring is already upon us. I see the tortoises, or rather I hear them drop from the bank into the brooks at my approach. The catkins of the alders have blossomed. The pads are springing at the bottom of the water. The pewee is heard, and the lark."
— Henry David Thoreau, *Journal*, March 30, 1851

Thoreau's love for and close observation of nature while rambling through woods, fields, pastures, wetlands, and country thoroughfares (Thoreaufares?) has inspired generations of naturalists and environmentalists. His spirit of activism bookended his quiet reflections and skill in slow, careful observation of the phenology of the planet, such as when flowers bloom and songbirds arrive in spring. His legacy has driven many people to dedicate their lives to the study of plants and animals. He is considered by many to be one of the founders of environmentalism.

As a director of field stations and marine labs, I have been fortunate to travel around the world to visit and consult with fellow field station directors, scientists, conservationists, and land managers over the past twenty years. Every day I see Thoreau's teachings personified. They live in the heart of an undergraduate student using a waterproof video camera in a marsh to observe crabs feeding on submerged saltmarsh cordgrass. I see that same intensity of concentration in a graduate student perched twenty feet up a tree looking for arboreal birds like yellow-throated vireos or identifying the beetles that live within the bark. Post-doctoral students roaming blackened hillsides in the west after megafires, looking for regrowth, carry his words in their back pockets.

The science of phenology has shown us how plants and animals adapt to a warming climate and changes in seasons, and how pollinators and the plants they visit have missed each other like ships passing in the night. Even during the pandemic, field stations and marine labs sprang into action to create virtual visits to our habitats so that homebound students could practice their observational skills.

Thoreau would be pleased that thousands of natural areas are protected around the world, from single acres in urban areas around St. Louis to sessional forests in New York State to hundreds of hectares in African savannah, primarily for the purpose of studying and contemplating nature.

He would be displeased at the fact that, so many years later, the rights of all people to clean air, water, and access to nature are not guaranteed. While writing in his journal, just a few paragraphs after the sentence above, he was decrying the treatment of enslaved people in the U.S. and the unjustness and immorality of the Fugitive Slave Act of 1850.

Who will be our next Thoreau? Who will inspire the next generation of students to spend time in the woods on long rambles looking for the first flowers of spring? Who will stand up for injustice and the environment? Fortunately, when I teach, I encounter college classes full of students who care about environmental justice, indigenous environmental knowledge, and combating climate change. A 2018 Gallup poll found a "global warming age gap" in concern and risk perceptions for Americans. Specifically, 70% of adults aged 18 to 34 say they worry about global warming compared to 62% of those between the ages of 35 and 54 and 56% of those aged 55 or older.

The environmental justice movement focuses on remediation and protection for the people who live in America's most polluted environments — often people of color and the poor. Student leaders like Greta Thunberg have inspired an army of student activists who speak in their parliaments, on the streets of Uganda and Laos, or in the schools of California demanding environment action. Groups like the Sunrise Movement, Zero Hour, Extinction Rebellion, Earth Guardians, and the International Youth Climate Movement are youth-led organizations mobilizing across the globe. They are pushing for action on the Green New Deal and the Civilian Climate Corps as well as providing a young voice for the United Nations' Conference of the Parties. Henry would be impressed.

Henrik Otterberg *is an economist at the Johanneberg Science Park in Gothenburg, Sweden. He wrote his Ph.D. on Thoreau's aesthetics in 2014, and since 2017 serves on the Thoreau Society board of directors. He is also the reviews and bibliography editor for the* Thoreau Society Bulletin.

Meme — and Memorable Thoreau

Henrik Otterberg

Many of Thoreau's famous quotes are by now so ubiquitous that they tend to pass us by without prompting much reflection. Simplicity, wildness, the mass of men, and a different drummer. Akin to clichés, they have arguably become the victims of their own pithy success. More than anything, perhaps, they strike us latecomer afiçionados as brand slogans for what is by now an amorphous yet still somehow recognizable Thoreau-at-large — conveyed not only, or even primarily, by academia, but rather via popular culture in all its myriad manifestations.

While we may harbor some misgivings about the Thoreauvian super-entity thus (re)created in the public domain, we are generally happy to pack the reprint, wear the T-shirt, glue the sticker, and pocket the keychain, all carrying their catchy messages like K-Mart koans. As is the nature of any category growing to encompass more and more, however, it conversely comes to define — and single out — less and less. That Thoreau T-shirt you saw adorning a torso in the parking lot may have been worn by an environmentalist, anarchist, libertarian, or feminist; by a conservative or progressive; or yet again by a platonist or hedonist. Or indeed by some combination of the above. Thoreau-at-large contains, and embraces, multitudes.

Placing Thoreauvian quotes in new contexts may grant them novel and specific significance. Rather than hearing Thoreau distorted by countless overdubs, as we are often wont to do, we suddenly infer that we hear his personal, unadorned voice, speaking gently but insistently to us. It may also follow at such junctures that we pick up on other memorable Thoreau formulations, more directly addressed, as these now seem, to ourselves and our times.

The Covid-19 pandemic has foisted a range of new circumstances upon us, many of them having to do with restrictions and loss: the former of movement, of space, perhaps also of courage; the latter, at worst, of vocation, health, even loved ones. Simultaneously, and particularly in the USA, political polarization seems to have created an ideological and racial divide unseen since Civil War days.

A relatively out-of-the-way Thoreauvian quote I have appreciated mulling over lately with this backdrop in mind is his declaration, well into the "Economy" chapter of *Walden*, that "I desire that there may be as many different persons in the world as possible." This is a remarkable statement, first of all, to any who would infer that he advocated his own specific lifestyle or background over that of others. Here, to the contrary, Thoreau's intent is to convey the importance of individual choice over tradition and precedent.

Make your life a war against cliché! One finds a humorous riff on this in his Journal of March 21, 1840: "There is this moment proposed to me every kind of life that men lead anywhere, or that imagination may print. By another spring I may be a mail-carrier in Peru, or a South African planter, or a Siberian exile, or a Greenland whaler, or a settler on the Columbia river, or a Canton merchant, or a soldier in Florida, or a mackerel fisher off Cape Sable, or a Robinson Crusoe in the Pacific, or a silent navigator of any sea. So wide is the choice of parts."

Make active personal choices then, and follow your own genius, wherever it ends. This is what we infer Thoreau to be saying. But there is also the social dimension to his outlook. While he may not have chosen, ultimately, to carry mail in South America, plant in Africa, or pursue trade in the Far East, he nevertheless recognizes these as valid, alternate life choices and outcomes. In his *Walden* quote, Thoreau also admits to a preference for diversity: he desires that there be other people, other perspectives, and other lives than his own. We should thus respect and work for the freedom not only of ourselves, but actively for the freedom of others. For these freedoms are, as Thoreau reminds us, very much conjoined and interdependent.

Nicole Palmer *is a Nursing assistant and Geriatric consultant and a member of the Thoreau Farm Board of Trustees. She lives in Concord near Great Meadows with her son Morgan, daughter Olivia, and her dog Nina. She has spent the last half of her life renovating old houses. With a love for the poetry of Mary Oliver, she is naturally drawn to "all things Henry."*

Happiness and Henry

Nicole Palmer

"Goodness is the only investment that never fails."
— Henry David Thoreau, *Walden*

If Henry were here today, I think he would do just as he did in his day: live a good life! Henry, somehow, knew the secret to a good life and found it everywhere, or it found him. "Happiness is like a butterfly, the more you chase it, the more it will evade you, but if you notice the other things around you, it will gently come and sit on your shoulder." Henry made Happiness a choice and not an outcome of circumstance.

Henry focused on the good and went out looking for reasons to be happy. "I know of no more encouraging fact than the unquestionable ability of man to elevate his life by conscious endeavor." He found excitement and joy in nature and in simple pleasures. Henry's words were warm and loving: in a letter to Richard Fuller, he expressed his sincere appreciation for a music box, saying, "It seems to be playing just for us two pilgrims marching over hill and dale of a summer afternoon."

Practicing gratitude is acknowledging and being thankful for what we have received. It elicits positive attributes — spiritually, emotionally, and in our health and well-being. Henry appreciated every changing season, especially those "Autumnal Tints," and he pitied city-dwellers who never got to the country to experience them. Henry was surprised that English poetry missed the "brilliancy of our Autumnal Foliage." Henry didn't overlook those details. How easily we miss a sunset or pass by the beauty of a lake, without pausing to appreciate them. It is easy to take for granted all we have: the air we breathe, clean water, the roof over our heads. For some of us it takes a loss to gain real appreciation. But Henry paused, and practiced gratitude in all he did.

He lived wanting to experience all that life had to offer and not waste or miss out on any of life's glory. Being in Nature was easy for him and it brought him great joy, thereby enriching and guiding his life. Henry turned to Nature to learn what it had to teach. He also balanced many close relationships with a deep commitment to himself, to his own meditation and care.

Henry focused on personal goals and didn't compare himself to others. He was confident in who he was and what he wanted to achieve. He stated his desire "to be judged by his strengths and not compared to his classmates." And yet I've heard many people compare him to his dear friend Ralph Waldo Emerson — different in many ways but, like all good friends, mutually supportive.

Edward Emerson remembered Henry "as the best kind of older brother" and later as a guide and advisor. The Emerson children loved to hear stories of Henry's childhood and would run to hug him, his goodness evident. "With goodness comes strength and self-reliance." And moving to be alone in the woods, far from neighbors, takes self-reliance. Henry speaks of Solitude as a good companion and yet had the balance of those close friendships as well.

When Henry "went to the woods to live deliberately," maybe he meant in both practical and philosophical terms. When leaving Walden, he said he had more lives to live, and for many of us he is still living them, in the legacy he left us.

How did this Concord boy, so like any other boy, take to a life in search of Happiness? I believe that, as he came to the end of his life, he felt it was everything he had hoped it to be. Deciding to live with gratitude, goodness, and self-reliance, being present in his relationships, and looking outside himself may have been a combination of instinct and discipline. Whatever the reason, it brought him Happiness.

When asked by his aunt, in his final weeks, "if he had made peace with God" he replied, "I did not know we had ever quarreled."

How did Henry know all this before the internet? It has taken me two years in a pandemic to find the components to Happiness. How did *you* decipher them, my Walden Prophet?

Donna Marie Przybojewski *is a teacher at St. Benedict Catholic School in Garfield Heights, Ohio, whose mission is to make Thoreau accessible to children. She is also the author/ illustrator of seven children's books on Thoreau, three of which have been used as story walks at Walden Pond State Reservation.*

My Partner Teacher

Donna Przybojewski

What would Henry do with a group of junior high students who have experienced isolation, anxiety, bigotry, and fear during the past two years? My sixth, seventh, and eighth graders, who are primarily African American, have been unable to see classmates and teachers. They have experienced racism and have shared the financial stress of their parents who have lost jobs. Well, Henry would do what he always did — be himself and be empathetic to these adolescents, just as when he comforted Edward Emerson who became upset when he dropped his basket of huckleberries as a child. In an attempt to make my students realize their own worth and potential, Henry would say, "If I am not I, who will be?"

Therefore, I will rephrase the question. What did Henry do? For the past six years, Henry has been a strong influence in my students' lives since I introduced him extensively in my classes. He has developed a relationship with them as my unseen partner teacher in class. Through biographical information, the reading and discussion of *Walden*, his essays, and especially excerpts from journal entries, Henry revealed to my students that his life was an ordinary one. However, his life became extraordinary due to his perseverance through hardship, as well as his joy in a simple life without materialism. He demonstrated how to have courage, how to stand up for justice, and how not to let the words of others curtail what he wished to accomplish.

Students at this age tend to be reluctant to express their emotions to adults, especially in the classroom setting. Henry, however, created an atmosphere where they felt comfortable enough to share their fears. This has enabled me, as their Language Arts teacher, to help my students think critically and develop enough self-esteem to confront the problems encountered in their young lives.

Since my students know the whole Henry and not just parts of him, as the nature writer, social activist, philosopher, and surveyor, he was able to guide them to understand his words at a much deeper level. He helped them realize that they, too, are not defined by their race, gender, successes, failures, athletic skills, or academic abilities.

Because of their comfort level with Henry, students engaged in open discussion about the bigotry they encountered. They shared experiences of being followed in stores because of their race, being called names, and being told they did not belong. Students then read negative remarks made about Henry during his life. He demonstrated that the words of others need not affect the success of one's life. Since many of my students have experienced loss — some through gun violence — learning of Henry's losses of a brother, sister, and father showed them that life can still be vital. Even Henry's suffering in the final months of his life demonstrated to my students that their lives have meaning beyond the suffering.

Henry has also shown my students how to live a just life and modeled how they could develop into individuals of integrity and moral decency. He taught them that no one's life is insignificant by introducing them to individuals who lived on the fringes of his society, such as Brister Freeman and Cato Ingraham in *Walden*.

"What would Henry do with my junior high students?" I respond with what he *has done*. He showed them how important it is to contribute to a community in a positive way through his abolitionist activities. Henry demonstrated concern for the most vulnerable through his compassion for Johnny Riordan, giving the Irish boy his coat since the child had none. He revealed that material items do not bring happiness, and he exemplified the importance of listening to one's own conscience and doing what is right by spending a night in jail when he protested a tax that contributed to slavery.

Why is this important? It is important because sometimes we only see the outward demeanor of students until this type of sharing occurs. Such sharing allows for a new mutual understanding and encourages us to be compassionate and empathetic. It helps us see that we are not alone in the midst of the difficult world we live in but have each other to lend support.

Yes, my students have learned much from Henry. They know what he would have done during the past two tumultuous years. He has encouraged them to think critically about their values and actions. He has shown them to "follow their own drummers," to be the change that they envision for their world, and to continually ask, "What would Henry do?"

Photo Credit: Irena Roman

John Roman *is a regular contributor to* Artists Magazine *and has written for several other national art magazines. Roman's Thoreau-related essays have appeared in* The Bungalore Review, Electrum Magazine, *and* The Concord Saunterer. *A graduate of Suffolk University's New England School of Art & Design, John has been teaching at the Massachusetts College of Art and Design in Boston since 1993. He is the author of* 50 Markets of Illustration *and* The Art of Illustrated Maps.

Henry Visits 2022

John Roman

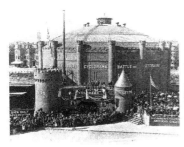

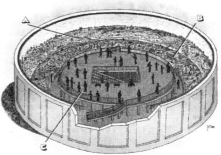

During the 1800s many cities worldwide hosted Cycloramas. In Boston, hundreds of patrons line the streets on opening day of "The Battle of Gettysburg" exhibit.

A Cyclorama displaying a 400-foot-long by 50-foot-high 360-degree panoramic painting: (A) Painting (B) Diorama (C) Viewing Platform (*Illustration by the author*)

Cyclorama Building, Battle of Gettysburg. Tremont Street, Boston, MA ca. 1855–1895. Courtesy Boston Public Library.

Thoreau's time had its own form of what's referred to today as "virtual reality." In major cities around the world, people flocked to Cycloramas, large circular buildings which housed immense 50-foot-high paintings that spread out to 400 feet in width. The enormous paintings were wrapped around the interior walls and surrounded viewers in an all-encompassing 360 degrees. The realism of the paintings was further enhanced by 3-D dioramas in the foreground which included carefully staged objects, landscaping, and mannequin figures scaled to merge with the background art. From an elevated platform in the center of the auditorium, patrons could roam, observe, and become immersed in a realistic panorama on display.

Produced at uniform sizes, cyclorama shows circulated from city to city and were featured in identically-built theaters. A wide variety of cyclorama themes included topics on history and folklore, notable battles, tours of Europe, and even taking visitors back in time to sites like ancient Rome or on location to the crucifixion of Christ.

True manipulators of escapism, cyclorama artists created exhibitions with such a degree of believability it was reported that 19th century audiences were held in a state of aesthetic arrest. People often recounted having difficulty keeping in mind they were merely looking at a painting and came away convinced that, while inside the cyclorama exhibit, they were physically present in a different place and time.

These days such claims seem like exaggerations. Nevertheless, a reliable eyewitness from the 1850s corroborated this fact. Henry David Thoreau, in his essay "Walking," recorded the following testimony after he visited one such cyclorama:

"Some months ago, I went to see a panorama of the Rhine. It was like a dream of the Middle Ages. I floated down its historic stream in something more than imagination, under bridges built by Romans, and repaired by later heroes, past cities and castles whose very names were music to my ears, and each was the subject of a legend. I floated along under the spell of enchantment, as if I had been transported to a heroic age…"

Considering Henry's unconventional concepts regarding linear time, it's understandable why the Rhine cyclorama kindled the illusion of being transported to an earlier age in history. For example, one account in his journal states, "Why does not God make some mistake to show us that time is a delusion?" Similarly, Henry's poem in *A Week on the Concord and Merrimack Rivers* refers to the ancient world and proclaims, "Where is the spirit of that time, but in the present day." And in *Walden*, Henry tells the story of a woodcarver who abolishes time while creating a staff.

Let us, then, follow this premise of the spirit of all times being alive "in the present day," and visualize Henry being transported to the spirit of a *future* time … *our* time, by way of a 19th-century cyclorama that depicts the year 2022. There is no need to describe what Henry sees as he walks the platform and peers into the 21st century. We know what Henry sees, and we imagine he comprehends all the problems we face. But, to answer the question "What would Henry *do*?" ... the answer would have to be, "There is nothing else he can do for us now." Henry already did everything he could when he poured his wisdom, philosophies, and advice into numerous books, essays, and journal entries. As Henry made clear in *A Week*, he and every other author speaks, "...not only to those who have gone before, but to those who may come after." In other words, Henry's writings, though penned nearly two hundred years ago, are what he contributes to the world today.

Thankfully, there are dedicated scholars, journalists, and authors among us who are picking up where Henry left off. These are the "Henrys" of our modern age, writers who are speaking to us in the present and will, like Henry, speak to those who come after us. For certain, this, too, Henry sees in the cyclorama exhibit of 2022, and he's honored his legacy is being carried on in our heroic age.

Rob Salafia *is an authority on executive presence and transformative learning experiences. He combines two decades of experience as a top leadership development executive with a successful career in the performing arts. He is the author of* Leading from Your Best Self: Develop Your Executive Poise, Presence and Influence to Maximize Your Potential *(McGraw-Hill). As a learning partner and workshop facilitator, Rob has worked with Fortune 500 companies including, PepsiCo and American Express. As an executive coach, Rob finds great satisfaction in guiding leaders through transitions to more senior roles, as well as coaching senior executives and leadership teams to enhance team effectiveness and prepare for strategic presentations.*

Rob is a lecturer at MIT Sloan School of Management and an MIT Leadership Center Master Executive Coach. Rob has a Master's degree from Boston University in Administration and Organizational Policy, as well as a Graduate Certificate in Executive Coaching from William James College. He is certified in the PRINT assessment on unconscious motivators.

Seeking Meaning and Purpose in Your Work?
Henry Would've Said "Be Like Water"

Rob Salafia

Henry Thoreau is often thought of as a dilettante, or 19th-century hippie, shirking a professional career and only working when he had to, most famously as a surveyor on a job-by-job basis. It's true that he worked just enough to pay bills while keeping such bills as few and far between as possible.

But Henry *did* pursue a career as a writer, and he worked hard at it. Though *Walden* and his other books didn't sell many copies during his lifetime, they do now, 160 years after his death. His writing ultimately influenced the major thinkers of our time, including Robert Frost who proclaimed: "In one book, he surpasses everything we have had in America."

Bruce Lee, the legendary martial artist, may have best articulated the strategic path to career success that characterized Henry's approach to finding a purposeful work life when he said, "Be like water." Lee explained, "Water flows in an endless quest for the sea. No matter the obstacle, water always finds a way, without force and without conflict. It finds the most efficient path to its goal. To be reunited. To belong."

So how might Henry decide on a career if he were here today? And how can each of us do the same? My own life journey offers some clues:

In college I became a geographer with a focus on International Development. I was studying Nepal, the border country between India and China. By junior year I was flying to Kathmandu for a semester abroad. It was 1975 so very little development had reached this remote Himalayan country. It was an extraordinary four-month experience. I lived with a native family next to a Tibetan Buddhist monastery, taught English in a village school, and trekked close to the base camp of Mount Annapurna.

It was when I returned home that things got difficult. The career path that was being laid out for me was in direct conflict with my Nepal experience. I was at a crossroads and had no one to help me sort it out. I finished school with no defined career path ahead and decided to chart one of my own.

The result was a left-hand turn into theater. Juggling, to be more specific. This appealed to my sense of adventure, as Nepal had. I immersed myself in the world of theater. I enrolled in a theater school for performers and was introduced to a community of like-minded artists. Lessons came right away and not always in a formal manner.

One morning, in the large red barn where we took our classes, I was facing a wall juggling three Indian clubs. Without announcement, the teacher entered the barn and started to walk past me, then he stopped, looked at me, and made a comment. "Salafia," he said, "you just don't look like a juggler." And then he walked away.

His comment shocked me at first, but then his words began to penetrate deeper. It didn't matter that I could juggle the clubs, my teacher didn't see me as a juggler. At that moment I got hooked. I found my path. One where I knew I could make a difference and where I had an identity. I was a juggler and had to look and feel like one!

Today, so many years later, I am an executive coach and have found my purpose as a catalyst for personal transformation. I now look and feel like a different kind of juggler, one that helps people make sense of their lives. I found mine and so can you.

Do you have a vision for your life and career? Do you feel it right down deep inside of you? Was it a long-time dream? Or, like Henry and me, did you get hooked on a branch that was sticking out along the bank of the river as you floated down.

Be like water, Bruce Lee said. Find a place you can go and keep going until you are overflowing with meaning and purpose. Henry did it way back then. I did it in our own time. Now it's your turn.

Heidi Jon Schmidt *is the author of* The Harbor Master's Daughter, The House on Oyster Creek, *and* The Rose Thieves, *among others. Her stories and essays have been published in the* New York Times, The Atlantic, Grand Street, *and* Yankee Magazine, *and have been featured on National Public Radio. She has won awards including the O. Henry, the Ingram-Merrill, and the James Michener.*

Would Henry Go Mad?

Heidi Jon Schmidt

A large, and surprisingly well-organized, group of our fellow citizens are working on many fronts to do nothing less than destroy our understanding of objective truth, and our laws with it. An insurrection that came within inches of killing our elected leaders on January 6, 2021, is dismissed by some of those same leaders as "a typical tourist day" in D C. In some states it's illegal to speak the words "climate change." Others are rushing to legislate any mention of racism out of their history curriculum.

A purportedly leftist group, whose ads for Green Party candidates reached hundreds of thousands of voters in 2018, was actually funded by the rightwing organization Turning Point, with the aim of splitting the Democratic vote.

Turning Point used a tool that would boggle Thoreau's mind: Facebook, whose algorithms can pinpoint every bias; every weakness of mind; can sell tyrants to those who crave authority; piety to the sanctimonious; even a sense of individuality to those who dream of standing bravely alone.

At Stanford Law School in June 2021, the Federalist Society, a group of Ouija board enthusiasts who claim to know and act on the deepest thoughts of our nation's founders, attempted to deny one student the right to graduate because he had satirized the group in a pamphlet purporting to support the insurrection. The students who brought the claim, all headed for prestigious clerkships with conservative judges, said this student had defamed them, harmed the Society and their individual reputations.

The Federalist Society is a group of well-heeled white men, who therefore naturally command authority and are funded by incredibly deep pockets in their quest to make sure white men continue to reign supreme. Their news makes the *New York Times*, and has now remade the Supreme Court. Their claims, no matter how absurd, are taken seriously, and they had Stanford University high-stepping to their tune.

It was enough to send this author to her own Ouija board: what would Henry do? In these times one voice screams in the wilderness of mass media; in his, there was little way to get an important message out. He read his speech on behalf of John Brown to a small audience gathered in Concord.

And it is thought to have changed the course of history, to have stiffened the spines of abolitionists, who had been ready to disavow Brown and instead marched to war with his name on their lips.

A lone voice still can, and does, make a difference. When 17-year-old Darnella Frasier saw George Floyd arrested, she followed a journalist's natural impulse and recorded the entire nine-minute torture on a video that became the essential document in a murder trial that both revealed the depth of institutional racism in this country, and became one step toward addressing it.

In a time when our Republican officials are often comfortable lying; when propaganda and disinformation stream easily into the news; when even our most revered newspapers seem to tailor their reporting to exploit division; truth is still recognizable. We hear it in Joe Biden's measured voice. We saw it, unbearably, in Darnella Frazier's video.

The Pulitzer Prize committee has awarded Frazier a special citation for courageous reporting, which is courageous in itself, at a time when an institution like Stanford allows itself to be cowed. One 17-year-old did more to change the course of history than all the king's men. Thoreauvian.

Ben Shattuck, *a graduate of the Iowa Writers' Workshop, is a recipient of the PEN/Robert J. Dau Short Story Prize and a 2019 Pushcart Prize. He is the director of the Cuttyhunk Island Writers' Residency. His writing can be found in the* Harvard Review, The Common, the Paris Review Daily, Lit Hub, *and* Kinfolk Magazine. *He lives with his wife and daughter on the coast of Massachusetts, where he owns and runs a general store built in 1793.*

Gardens

Ben Shattuck

In the early morning, in the winter, Los Angeles is beautiful.
The rare clouds are decorative only, like strips of watery white
paint drawn across a blue page. It's very quiet before the cars
have started filling the streets — so quiet that, from my bedroom
window, I can hear the whir of hummingbirds' wings tracing
through the palms and loquat trees, bougainvillea, and marigolds
around my house. You get the impression that — with the
sheer amount of greenery between the concrete — if we all
disappeared tomorrow, this city would fold back to wilderness
faster than most. On my block, a tangle of nasturtiums has
grown up and over the sidewalk, from the rim of dirt around
a stop sign. And I have watched a small monarch butterfly
migration drift down the street, seemingly oblivious of the city,
as if they were passing over a wild field in Montana. And, a
mountain lion, caught between two highways and skulking in
my neighborhood every night last week, was filmed by security
cameras and became a national news story. In this city, I notice
the details of nature more than I do in my rural hometown back
in Massachusetts, because here nature's contours show so clearly
against — well, everything else.

It was on one of these early mornings that I drove twenty
minutes from my house, in east Los Angeles, to the Huntington
Gardens in Pasadena. The Huntington is a former estate of a
turn-of-the-century railroad magnate, and is now home to themed
gardens filled with show-stopping plants spread across 130 acres.
There's a bamboo forest, a Shakespeare Garden, a Japanese
tea house near a dozen bonsai, a rose garden, a desert garden,
a miniature habitat of Australia, and some of the weirdest and

brightest flowers I've ever seen. When somebody visiting LA asks me where to go, I suggest the Huntington, and only recently realized that I was telling them, in a way, to leave the city they'd decided to visit.

The Huntington Museum also houses some literary treasures: a Gutenberg Bible; Audubon's *Birds of America* elephant folio; a letter from Walt Whitman after visiting his brother in a Civil War hospital; Sir Isaac Newton's scribbles about alchemy (along with his death mask); and, I think the most fitting for museum placed in the middle of gardens, the handwritten pages of *Walden*. The page of *Walden* under the display glass is, oddly, not the first or last or even the most inspiring: it is from "Economy," and is Thoreau's thoughts on clothing. "The object of clothing, first, is to retain the body's heat, and second, in the state of society, to cover nakedness," he wrote, in his open and painterly cursive.

After I left the cool and cavernous building, blinking in the midmorning sun, I walked to a shady section of the tropical gardens. I sat on a grassy slope. A mockingbird called nearby. The wind was strong that day, and the palm fronds rattled like streamers overhead — altogether sounding like rain coming down on a roof. I rested on my back, thought about Henry David Thoreau, about his handwriting I'd just seen on display, and about the project he'd set out for himself when he was so young, only in his late twenties: "I went to the woods because I wished to live deliberately," he famously wrote. I thought of what he eventually stood for and against, in the tide of events and crimes and moral dilemmas streaming through his brief life.

What was streaming through my life? What was the news of the day, while I sat listening to the mockingbird and the rattling palms? Simply, many environmental and humanitarian catastrophes: war in Ukraine; a hunger crisis in Afghanistan; another report of collapsing ecosystems; the pandemic newly tearing through another population; and a report on racial inequality within the pandemic. All these things, individually, would be topics that Henry David Thoreau might fervently respond to. Each one was so big, casting such a large shadow over the smallness of one person's opinion.

What would he do when our screen-filled world bombards us with bad news from every corner of the earth? One answer, the hopeful answer, is that he would protest. He would be online, writing about climate change, pacifism, racial justice, and the environmentalist ideals. Then, I thought of his desire to leave 'the village' behind. I thought of the man who walked no less than four hours a day and fed a mouse by hand and recorded the arrival of flowers in the spring as if they were friends he were welcoming home. I wondered if he might, instead, leave the writing desk, the computer, social media, the internet all behind — preferring instead to find a shady spot in a garden, taking in what pleasures he could, staring up at the feathered clouds painting the sky.

Scott Slovic is *University Distinguished Professor of Environmental Humanities at the University of Idaho. His teaching includes fully analog writing courses in the Semester in the Wild Program that takes place in the Frank Church River of No Return Wilderness. He served as founding president of the Association for the Study of Literature and Environment (ASLE) in the early 1990s, and from 1995 to 2020 he was the editor-in-chief of* ISLE: Interdisciplinary Studies in Literature and Environment. *His many books include* Seeking Awareness in American Nature Writing: Henry Thoreau, Annie Dillard, Edward Abbey, Wendell Berry, Barry Lopez; *and* Numbers and Nerves: Information, Emotion, and Meaning in a World of Data.

Look, Listen, Write

Scott Slovic

We live during a time of increasing abstraction. This is old news. For years, we've been reflecting on the emotional and cognitive implications of the internet, our reliance on the web for all forms of information. We long ago abandoned paper letters, for the most part, and leaned in on email and Facebook Messenger. For those of us who are teachers, Zoom and other platforms began to replace face-to-face classes in March 2020, shortly after the Covid-19 pandemic reached American shores.

During this time of increasingly virtual living, I have often asked myself, "What would Thoreau do … if he were alive at this time?" There are plenty of clues in his writing.

My colleague William Major wrote "Thoreau's Cellphone Experiment" for *The Chronicle of Higher Education* in 2011, describing an exercise he conducted with his undergraduates, for which he invited students to earn extra-credit by giving him their smartphones and BlackBerries (remember those?) for five days, freeing them to heed Thoreau's "calls for simplicity and solitude," conditions of life that seem essentially out of reach when we're constantly checking our digital devices.

I have often conducted Thoreauvian experiments in my own writing classes, encouraging students and workshop participants to heighten their awareness of the more-than-human world and their own bodily presence in the world, while at the same time stepping away, at least briefly, from the anxiety inevitably spawned by daily news of a society in meltdown and a burning-drowning planet.

There is solace in paying attention. This is something anyone who practices meditation will confirm.

Rather than asking my students to meditate in a traditional way, emptying their minds or focusing on a verbal koan, I invite them to notice the world. I use Henry's journal, which he kept almost daily from 1836 to 1861, as a model for my own students' writing. When Henry hit his stride as a journal-writer, he often elided his own presence in the scenes he recorded, avoiding the pronoun "I" and sinking his attention in the physical world around him. Henry's quintessential journal entry is the three-word statement for October 6 and 7, 1853: "Windy. Elms Bare." To me, this statement captures the swinging branches of elm trees, bare of leaves as fall becomes winter. An entire scene and state of mind articulated in a few spare words.

Other entries capture color and movement with a richness that defies the abstraction many of us experience as the dominant state of our 21st-century lives. On October 4, 1853, Henry wrote: "The maples are reddening, and birches yellowing. The mouse-ear in the shade in the middle of the day, so hoary, looks as if the frost still lay on it. Well it wears the frost. Bumblebees are on the *Aster undulatus*, and gnats are dancing in the air."

I like to think that if Henry were still around, and if he had a forum for reaching out to students or to the broader public, he might suggest that others practice close observation and journal-writing as antidotes to the bodiless abstraction of our daily lives. He might say, "Close your email, step outside, look carefully at the leaves in colorful transition, listen to the wind, and take a few notes — immerse yourself in the material world and savor the existence of your body in the world." My students report that this simple exercise is mind-blowing.

In so many ways, the cyberworld is extraordinarily efficient and empowering. Lecturing over Zoom has begun to replace physical travel to distant conferences. Despite the need for electricity to power our computers and internet servers, we may be able to mitigate our use of fossil fuels by transferring some aspects of our lives to the virtual realm. But we remain, as Scott Russell Sanders eloquently put it in "Speaking a Word for Nature," "animals, two-legged sacks of meat and blood and bone dependent on the whole living planet for our survival." To drive this idea home, Henry might suggest that we take the time, now and then, to truly inhabit our senses and then reinforce the experience by writing a brief description — to be deeply present in the world.

Kim Stafford *is the founding director of the Northwest Writing Institute at Lewis & Clark College and author of twenty books of poetry and prose, including* Singer Come from Afar *(Red Hen Press, 2021). www.kimstaffordpoet.com*

Walden on the Mountain

Kim Stafford

When I was given time at a cabin on a headland by the sea, I thought it could be my Walden. I would write wonders, so I brought all this paper, unloading bushels of writing drafts, reference books, and computer equipment I had with me. By then it was night, and through the window I noticed the full moon, and — needing to live deliberately — stepped outside.

Standing in the gloom of the spruce forest there, I remembered a moment years before at the Root Feast, the Native version of Thanksgiving that I had witnessed at the Warm Springs Indian Reservation, two hundred miles to the east. The drums, the dance, the singing — and then the feasting — all took the better part of a day. But there was one moment that came to me under the moon. The drumming had suddenly stopped, and an old man stepped to the microphone before the seven silent Washat drummers.

"I went down to the corner," he called out, "to see if there might be a song — waiting to see if anyone could hear it! I have heard it! I would sing it for you." And he began to sing, in the Sahaptin language, the song that had come to him, as the drums began again behind him.

As I remembered that moment, I realized there might be a song waiting for me that night, somewhere up on the mountain. I needed to leave my papers and my plans, and be here, this night, this chance.

The forest path led me up from the cabin, through dense forest, and then west, across open meadows, to the peak of the headland that fronts the sea. With my little flashlight and notebook, I started up the steep climb, turning where shadowy trees gestured large against my light, the city receding from my mind. Modern time ebbed away. My intentions dwindled. And I began to remember immediate things.

I remembered how the river, at the foot of the headland, flows north out of its estuary, and then makes a bold turn to the west where it meets salt water. I remembered that spruce trees, being carbon structures, are made of air, literally built of the sea wind they inhale. I remembered seeing the salmon in the creek, just below my residence, thrashing in shallow water to build the redd of gravel where they would then spawn and die. I remembered the vocation behind all my plans: to be a citizen who writes for the healing of the world.

Then, steaming from the climb, I was at the trail's farthest western point, where the sea spread out hundreds of feet below, glittering in the moonlight, where the surf beat its plush rhythm in the cove. The far, amber lights of crab boats glowed dim in the dark. Behind me, an owl called. Then the world was so still, I could hear my heart. And then I heard the song.

I am not talking about inspiration, magic, the muse. I am talking about the way a simple song is waiting to be heard from somewhere behind the quiet desperation of many days. It started with syllables from the place: River turns … wind returns … tree tangles … sun spangles … vagabond salmon, home again … leave your bones among the stones and travel in your dream.

I felt like an otter, frisky with thought, calm with plenty, not knowing time as a monolith to design, but as a fluid, ever-present river to explore and to savor.

When I stood up and turned from the sea, it was after midnight, and I had the bones of a song in my mind, and a few lines scrawled in my notebook. My boxes of paper, and my loom of computer cables, were poised in the dark cabin. Time stretched before me. Time and the song.

Editor's note: *"Walden on the Mountain" was adapted from a note posted on the website of the Alliance for Artist Communities.*

Robert Sullivan *is the author of such books as* Rats, The Meadowlands, *and* The Thoreau You Don't Know. *He is a contributing editor to* A Public Space, *the literary magazine; an instructor at Middlebury College's Bread Loaf School of English; and a 2021 Guggenheim Fellow. He lives in Philadelphia.*

So-called Peace

Robert Sullivan

What he would do is go out in a boat (or try to) or take a walk and look around — look for signs of spring, always his favorite season, so much so that he could find signs of it any day of the year. He would maybe make some sketches, clip some flowers, if he could find some. He would be distressed at the monotony that has taken over in the New England forests, and the loss of meadows and attendant bugs and birds would hurt. The monolith that is the American roadway would probably send him into shock, though it would send anybody from the 19th century into shock, and at rush hour on a hotter-than-previously-recorded climate-warmed day, it could send you into shock too — literally, if you stood out on the shoulder of I-95 for too long. In the cities, he would be fascinated by things growing in so-called abandoned lots, and just typing *abandoned*, it's hard not to imagine his reaction. "Abandoned by whom?" he would ask. Concord was emptying out when he was alive, so he'd understand quickly that the city was not abandoned by the people who lived there so much as the people who lived there were abandoned by the bank and the city and the state.

When he asked who lived there — whose neighborhoods were abandoned — we'd have to get around to the Civil War, which had begun in July of 1861, when Thoreau was entering his last throes of tuberculosis, less than a year from his death. "Thoreau, sadly out of health, was the only cheerful man in Concordia," reported Moncure Daniel Conway, a Boston abolitionist. That summer, the North had begun to understand that the war was not going to be over in a matter of months. Thoreau read this as the North taking action at last. "[H]e was in a state of exaltation," Conway noted, "about the moral regeneration of the nation."

If you were to book Thoreau on the *Today* show ("Coming up, a chat with a back-to-the-land pioneer, and then the summer blockbuster everyone's talking about …") or for an interview with the *New York Times* ("We sat down for a lunch of locally grown greens to get his take on tiny houses, zero-carbon airlines, and the new breed of celebrity climate activists …"), then you'd notice that while the interviewers were asking for his take on global warming, he'd be asking you about the war.

You'd tell him it was over, of course, that Union troops beat the Confederates, but he'd ask questions. You'd mention that while Reconstruction started out with good intentions, the North, with the encouragement of Northern politicians and businessmen, withdrew the troops necessary to enforce it, thereby looking away as a guerilla war was waged against the formerly enslaved, who, in the North *and* the South, were now confined in what were called ghettos (even if they weren't) and murdered mercilessly, their neighborhoods eventually circled in red by the government and then "abandoned" until the banks and developers returned to develop the old neighborhoods away.

Thoreau would notice quickly that it sounds like the South won. As he learned that goods are bought and sold at a one-click pace that has the smell of military logistics, and that energy companies attack the earth to power a mechanized world that only devours itself further, he'd say it sounds as if there's still a war going on.

It's not likely people would hear this. People don't think of Thoreau and war. They think of him as a prophet of non-violence, even though he fervently supported John Brown's violent action at Harpers Ferry, even though those who have studied Thoreau's tax protest have eventually supported more violent action as non-violence failed.

In 1967, after the summer rebellions, Martin Luther King said: "Let us say boldly that if the violations of law by the white man in the slums over the years were calculated and compared with the law-breaking of a few days of riots, the hardened criminal would be the white man. These are often difficult things to say but I have come to see more and more that it is necessary to utter the truth in order to deal with the great problems that we face in our society."

"We preserve the so-called peace of our community by deeds of petty violence every day," Thoreau said, in his speech defending John Brown. "Look at the policeman's billy and handcuffs! Look at the jail! Look at the gallows! Look at the chaplain of the regiment! We are hoping only to live safely on the outskirts of *this* provisional army."

Thoreau delivered the speech over and over in 1859, just before Brown was hanged. Were he around for his 205th birthday, he would very likely wish to read it again.

Mark Thoreau is a distant cousin of Henry David Thoreau and lives in the county of Sussex in the United Kingdom. He has had a keen interest in his family history since the age of 15 and joined the Thoreau Society at that time. As well as regular visits to Concord, Massachusetts, Mark regularly travels to the Channel Island of Jersey where the Thoreaus come from and enjoys spending time researching in the island's archive and Société Jersiaise. Mark is married to husband Stephen and they have a Labrador called Scooby.

Question Authority

Mark Thoreau

"I heartily accept the motto, 'That government is best which governs least'; and I should like to see it acted up to more rapidly and systematically. Carried out, it finally amounts to this, which also I believe, — 'That government is best which governs not at all' and when men are prepared for it, that will be the kind of government which they will have."
— Henry David Thoreau, "Civil Disobedience," 1849

March 23, 2020 is one of those dates that here in the United Kingdom will be cemented in our memory. On that date, we went into lockdown; businesses stopped trading; aircraft stopped flying; the daily commute was replaced with home working; and a new word was born to the UK — Furlough!

Overnight everything stopped: no cars on the road, no socializing, one hour of outside exercise allowed per day. Television and radio were plagued with scores of adverts telling us what to do, when we could do it, and for how long. At 5 p.m. each night, we were drawn to the television to listen to the daily government briefing, where slogans and figures were put on slideshows and presented to us, the public. The government had taken control of our lives.

The situation made me wonder: What would Henry do, say, or think about this new world we have been thrown into?

It's hard to say exactly what Henry would do in this situation as the world has changed in a multitude of ways since Henry passed away in 1862. While Slavery might no longer be an issue in the Western world, the fallout from slavery, systemic racism, and other social issues remain. Twenty-first-century humankind is also grappling with climate change, environmental issues, LGBTQ+ rights, our reliance on technology, and civil rights.

Henry would be socially responsible, use his common sense, and of course be suspicious of the government. Despite politicians not following the data and incorrect forecasts from government agencies, I have been shocked at how people have surrendered their freedoms to the state.

Where does this compliance come from? Could it be those television and radio announcements, or the 5pm government briefing? It has since come to light that a behavioral science sub group of SAGE (Scientific Advisory Group for Emergencies in the UK) published a paper the day before lockdown with recommendations for the type of language to be used to increase our adherence to the newly imposed measures. Using fear tactics, the level of public alarm was kept high. Signage everywhere reminded us to stay two meters apart, wash our hands, walk on the left, only enter a shop if the number of customers was under the permitted level, and wear a face covering. Like Henry, I suffer from defiance syndrome. If there is a rule, I just want to break it.

Our new way of living without liberty is causing an alarming increase in mental health issues. Where previously parents had discouraged children from spending too much time in front of a screen, they were now obliged to encourage it for remote schooling and Zoom calls with their friends. Children's education has been severely affected with lessons and examinations canceled or postponed. Domestic abuse is also on the rise.

My nephew questioned his schools' policy of not mixing year groups to prevent the spread of infection. All students in his year were put in a basketball court on their break, all three hundred of them! Was he right to question this? It has amazed me how, through fear, society has stopped questioning government policies, and how individuals have created their own interpretations.

It would appear that we have become obsessed with petty rules: neighbors calling the police if they have seen a visitor entering a house; seven people meeting up when the law states the maximum should be six; and the police fining two friends for meeting outside for a coffee. The restrictions on funerals are among the most consequential. In one instance in the UK, the proceedings were stopped as a son went to console his mother at her husband's funeral. Perhaps one of the saddest of these events was the Queen sitting on her own at Prince Phillips' funeral, even though the rules allowed her to sit next to her lady-in-waiting in the car on the way to the chapel.

When did we stop questioning our government? It's fair to say that in times of fear and concern, the public like clear guidance and rules from their government, and the government seems only too happy to oblige with those rules. As Henry said, "Any fool can make a rule, and every fool will mind it."

If the contradictory and confusing rules of government were not enough, we also have to deal with the misinformation that is spread from social media, in addition to a politically-biased press.

Henry would have approved of some of the societal changes that have taken place during the pandemic: taking a walk, whether alone or with friends, has become the new social event for people of all ages.

As Henry said, "It is a great art to saunter."

Apartments in cities have become less desirable as more people have opted to move to the country in pursuit of nature. Home baking and piecing together puzzles have become popular pastimes.

As we start to head towards the end of this pandemic and life slowly returns to normal, let's remember the positives and include them in our new lives.

Yet, as we make that move, the government is putting through new laws in its Police, Crime Sentencing, and Courts Bill. While there are many good elements of this bill, there is one small, but significant element that will give the police more powers to impose conditions on non-violent protests. Perhaps Henry was right to be suspicious of the government.

Robert M. Thorson *is a Midwestern native turned Northwestern geologist turned Northeastern academic. His immersion into the works of Henry D. Thoreau during the tumult of the late 1960s and early 1970s gave him a model to live by. He's a Professor of Geosciences at the University of Connecticut where he juggles teaching, scholarship, and service. Visiting scholarly appointments include Harvard University (American Studies), Universidad Tecnica de Santa Maria, Valparaiso, Chile (Civil Engineering), Dartmouth College (Geography), and Yale University (History). His pedestrian commute — being able to walk through the woods around a pond and upon a fieldstone wall to reach his lab and office at a research university — is an example of living deliberately. The last four of his seven books involve Thoreau Studies:* The Guide to Walden Pond; The Boatman: Henry David Thoreau's River Years; Walden's Shore: Henry David Thoreau and Nineteenth Century Science; *and* Beyond Walden: The Hidden History of America's Kettle Lakes and Ponds. *He is a father to four children and grandfather of three. His hobbies are reading, writing, walking, and cooking.*

Seeking Respite in Natural Science

Robert M. Thorson

What would Henry do about today's social and political issues? This depends on when in his lifetime we asked him. Statistically, this would have been during what I call his "wondrous decade" (1851-1861), the final, most stable, and most productive decade of his life.

Behind him lay his youthful unrequited loves, employment indecisions, sibling tragedies, seminary education, and idealism. Ahead lay his final protracted legal fight over the Billerica dam and his moral support for the radical abolitionist John Brown.

In this wondrous decade he had no debt to pay, no major project diverting his attention, no great excursions planned, and no great personal stressors. He was resolved to live a bachelor's life with his family on Main Street. His practice of land surveying and his employment in the family's graphite manufacturing business provided a reliable income. His third-floor sanctum offered a large and exceptionally private place to work as a naturalist. The mooring for his boat lay just across the street and less than one minute from his door, giving him almost instant access to thirty-three miles of navigable river. The railroad station was just around the corner and less than two minutes away, giving him convenient daily access to the intellectual resources of Harvard College in Cambridge and the Natural History Society in Boston, both of which could be reached within an hour. There he had unrestricted access to excellent libraries, museum collections, and knowledgeable colleagues.

All of this came together on September 7, 1851, when he finally declared his life purpose: "My profession is to be always on the alert to find God in nature, to know his lurking-places, to attend all the oratorios, the operas, in nature." Not wanting the dissipation of global travel, he committed himself to a life of natural science in Concord and vicinity, resulting in a journal so rich with sojourning observations that he proposed renaming it "Field Notes." Once in this groove, Thoreau rigorously and religiously followed a fairly regular pattern of reading in the evenings, journaling his thoughts in the morning, and sojourning on his rivers in the afternoons.

What would this fully mature and independent scientific thinker do with respect to today's environmental, political, and social issues?

Mostly, he would treat them as background noise, mere annoyances to otherwise perfect days. His self-declared profession was not to save the world, but to understand it through the tools of science, allowing him to appreciate the oratorios of God's nature in higher fidelity. But I can easily imagine his responses to our modern concerns.

Environmentally, he would remind us that "in Wildness is the preservation of the world." That the future of Earth as a habitable planet requires the intrinsic wildness of things beyond our control. Thoreau's pithy quote about wildness is his confession of faith in the higher power of Nature to create a post-Anthropocene afterlife. He would urge us to use less, spend less, travel less, and live with less clutter in our minds and homes.

Politically, he would remind us that politics works from the individual upwards. He previously described the higher politics of elected officials as the "gizzard of society" — a necessary, but dark place where nutritious individual ideas are ground up and turned into a lumpy, digestible paste. I think he would be appalled by the evening news, especially the financial debt we're taking on to prop up an economy based on the fallacy of endless growth. He would oppose the walls we keep building to maintain the arbitrary categories of humankind — nations, genders, races, ethnicities, classes, and whatnot — that divide us.

Socially, he would remind us that intervals of solitude are essential to good mental health. We must know ourselves as individuals before we can join a proper society devoted to the common good.

What would Henry do? During his wondrous decade of natural science, he surprised himself each day with something new. So, I wouldn't find it surprising today if we all got it wrong.

Nikki Turpin *(she/her/hers) is the Director of Diversity, Equity, and Inclusion at Chapel Hill-Chauncy Hall in Waltham, Massachusetts. Nikki sits on multiple Inclusivity and Diversity Boards including the Bay State Brawlers and Hudson Sloop Clearwater, and is a consultant for BeWellBeHere. She is the Programming Director for Robbins House in Concord, Massachusetts, and was the leader of the Youth in Philanthropy Program at Middlesex School for the Foundation for MetroWest. She has long held a passion for African-American history and presented at the Association of African American Museums, discussing the importance of telling the full stories of African-American female suffragists. She has presented and run Diversity, Equity, and Inclusion workshops at ACA New England, The National Humanities Conference, GLAD Legal Advocates and Defenders, Concord Recreation, Jewish Family and Children's Services, and Boys and Girls Clubs of Boston, leading their professional development and leadership institute. Nikki has worked in public, private, and independent education for over a decade.*

Care for a Cup of Tea?

Nikki Turpin

What would Henry think about us as a society? How we have abused the planet? How we have allowed man's greed to override any moral or empathetic feelings to care for each other? And how, almost 160 years after his death, Brown, Black, and indigenous people are still fighting for equality in a country that they built? Their bodies and minds are still abused and used as tools for the progress of others. They are still seen as a threat, and sadly, there are just too many people that look like Henry who don't care, or believe that the inequitable treatment is fine.

I can't help but believe that Henry, as an abolitionist, would be "throwing shade" at what he might perceive as performative social justice. The lawn signs, T-shirts, the black boxes on social media, all the things that are right but empty.

It's been a year since the murder of George Floyd and while there is small justice for his family, what has really changed when a child is shot directly in the chest later? There is continued pain and no change. There has not been the substantial change needed to make things better for all.

As Henry said, "It is not a man's duty, as a matter of course, to devote himself to the eradication of any, even the most enormous wrong; he may still properly have other concerns to engage him; but it is his duty, at least, to wash his hands of it, and, if he gives it no thought longer, not to give it practically his support."

I think of Ellen Garrison and how she sat in that segregated waiting room in a Baltimore train station and was "forcibly ejected." To risk one's life simply because it is the right thing to do is an honorable action. To care about your fellow humans in a way that risks your own mortality is exactly the selflessness that abolitionists modeled for us so long ago. They gave of themselves and now hold us and each other accountable for the changes we need to be a community of care and compassion. The Civil Rights Act of 1866 was law but the challenge was to ensure that it was practiced, not just another empty promise. Policy does not matter if we don't uphold it.

The Civil Rights movement of the 1960s did not fix America. In the Spring of 2020, there was a feeling of a "white awakening" but the commitments made have not been fulfilled. What's sad is that most of us knew they wouldn't be.

Where do we go from here?

In order for any of this to be fixed, you have to acknowledge that there is a problem, then you have to do something, anything! Small steps lead to big ones. Following that step is your next, and you will see yourself moving towards a world that is just and for all. Being an ally is the bare minimum; the next step is to be an active ally. That means calling out moments of bias in yourself and others, and sharing resources to guide uncomfortable conversations. Next is something I've said often: Be an accomplice. This means being proactive and not reactive. Challenge any biases, stereotypes, and injustice you see, no matter the source. Kick in the door for marginalized, oppressed, and culturally looted communities. Look around and ask why certain groups are or are not present. The pinnacle of this work is becoming a co-conspirator and with that comes constant vigilance in ensuring that all have a voice in your circle.

On July 23, 1846, Thoreau spent a night in jail, stating "I cannot for an instant recognize . . . as my government [that] which is the slave's government also."

I like to believe that had his tax not been paid for him he would have stayed in jail for as long as he felt necessary. He was at the co-conspirator level in a time when that role was not widely recognized or embraced.

What Would Henry Do? If Thoreau were here today, he would use his platform for Justice and Equity.

The real question is, what will we do?

Geoff Wisner *is a board member of the Thoreau Society. He is a book reviewer and essayist, the editor of* Thoreau's Animals, Thoreau's Wildflowers, *and* African Lives, *and the author of* A Basket of Leaves: 99 Books That Capture the Spirit of Africa. *He has given talks on Thoreau in the US, Norway, Portugal, and Sweden. He lives in New York City.*

Little Thoreaus Everywhere

Geoff Wisner

What would Henry do if he were alive today?

Before answering we may have to ask first, Who would Henry be if he were alive today? Who would he be if he had not been born "in the very nick of time" in a white frame house in 1817?

Can we imagine a 21st-century Thoreau who carries a cell phone and writes his essays on a laptop? Would he shop at a supermarket? Would he drive a car? Can we imagine a Thoreau who doesn't live in Concord, Massachusetts, "the most estimable place in all the world"?

There are some qualities, surely, that any kind of Henry David Thoreau must have. Thoreau reads deeply and writes deliberately. He loves nature and observes her both critically and ecstatically. He loves to walk. He requires a large dose of solitude. He gets along with children. He lives simply. Injustice angers him. His sense of humor is wicked but often overlooked.

The original Thoreau knew there was more than one way to live. "There is this moment proposed to me," he wrote in his Journal in 1840, "every kind of life that men lead anywhere, or that imagination can paint. By another spring I may be a mail-carrier in Peru, or a South African planter, or a Siberian exile, or a Greenland whaler, or a settler on the Columbia River, or a Canton merchant, or a soldier in Florida, or a mackerel-fisher off Cape Sable, or a Robinson Crusoe in the Pacific, or a silent navigator of any sea."

So why did he stay in Concord? Like so many things in life, it had a lot to do with money. In November 1853, as he finished his work on *Walden*, he wrote in the *Journal*, "I cannot but regard it as a kindness in those who have the steering of me that, by the want of pecuniary wealth, I have been nailed down to this my native region so long and steadily, and made to study and love this spot of earth more and more."

Yet "nailed down" as he was in Concord, he was determined to live more than one life there. Asking himself in 1852 why he no longer lived in the little house he built near Walden Pond, he wrote, "I do not think that I can tell … . Perhaps I wanted a change."

In the pages of *Walden* he was a little more definite. "I left the woods," he wrote, "for as good a reason as I went there. Perhaps it seemed to me that I had several more lives to live, and could not spare any more time for that one."

If you look around for present-day Thoreaus, they are not so hard to find. In Concord itself, Peter Alden can tell you which bird is calling in the Estabrook Woods, and Cherrie Corey can point out the marsh hibiscus blooming at Great Meadows. Margaret Carroll-Bergman lives in a tiny house on White Pond. Richard Smith and Brent Ranalli impersonate the man himself, dressing in Thoreau's homespun and answering questions in character. Maria Madison, through her work at Robbins House, places the story of Thoreau's Black neighbors in the context of the long struggle for civil rights.

But let's look a little more widely. Jeff VanderMeer writes fiction, a genre for which Henry had little use, but his passionate concern for plants and animals caused *The New Yorker* to call him "the weird Thoreau." Drew Lanham, Corina Newsome, and others are increasing the ranks of Black birders and nature lovers. E.O. Wilson's microscopic attention to the lives of the ants is nothing if not Thoreauvian. (Remember the battle of the ants in *Walden*.) Wangari Maathai founded the Green Belt Movement, empowering women in Kenya to plant trees and protect the environment.

These are the names we know, but there are many other modern-day Thoreaus, large and small, in Concord and around the world. Henry David Thoreau had no children, but he has many descendants.

Tanya Wright *is an award-winning actress, entrepreneur, and author. She has been an actor on critically acclaimed shows including Orange is the New Black, True Blood, NYPD BLUE, 24, ER, The Good Wife, and Madame Secretary. She got her start on The Cosby Show.*

Tanya received the Most Innovative Business Award from SOBRO for her haircare line, HAIRiette. Moved by the pandemic, Tanya pivoted the beauty line to focus on children and education. Hairiette of Harlem is a book about a spunky 7-year-old's adventures with her friend, Charlie the Talking Comb!

Tanya is pursuing a Master's degree at Harvard University's Graduate School of Education's Learning, Design Innovation and Technology program (2022) and building out various educational components of her brand in collaboration with the Harvard Innovation Lab.

Tanya is a native New Yorker.

Simply, Deliberately, Quietly

Tanya Wright

I was in my sophomore year at Vassar when I encountered a most interesting chap named Henry David Thoreau. Thoreau was sandwiched between Ralph Waldo Emerson, Walt Whitman, and Nathaniel Hawthorne in my American Literature class. I had a tendency to daydream in school (I was bored with school but would come full circle later) and wondered what it would be like to live in the woods for two years. The transcendentalists were all great but Thoreau seemed greater with his radical act of separating himself from society to live "**deliberately**, to front only the essential facts of life and learn what they had to teach and to discover if he had really lived."

It was a provocative concept juxtaposed with the excess of the time. I was a girl working to construct in my mind what my ideal reality would be after I graduated. There were lots of opinions all around about what I should do with my life, but during a daydream in Mr. DeMaria's literature class, something that was clear above all else was that I wanted to be happy. I didn't see most people around me prioritizing their happiness. What Thoreau did — and what I was about to do — seemed a radical act.

My junior year, still taken with this man with the long face and pointy nose, I decided to spend the bulk of my final semester on a thesis studying Thoreau's simple life more deeply. My work was a comparative study of literature of the 1840s, specifically, the worlds of two men — Henry David Thoreau and Frederick Douglass. While one was white and the other was Black, my thesis proved that these two men were far more alike than they were different.

If Thoreau were alive today, I imagine he would be dismayed by our consumerism and, above all, horrified at what we have done to our planet. He would urge us to shed the weight of our wants and to live simply. His voice would have a time rising to the top, though, because social media has taken up more space in our brains than should be allowed. Thoreau would be sad at the state of race relations in this country and lament how far there was still to go. He would be sickened to realize so many men still harbor such hatred for others who didn't look like them. I remember a colleague asked why I spent the bulk of my senior year on a thesis about a man who lived almost two centuries ago. "What did you think you were going to do with that?" they asked, as if one's thesis should have a purpose other than pure enjoyment, personal fulfillment, and the simple joy of learning. There was — and I imagine always will be — something peaceful in the words of *Walden*, a respite from a loud and noisy world. I believe it was Thoreau who helped give me the confidence to chart a rather unorthodox life of being an actor/writer and entrepreneur.

"Go confidently in the direction of your dreams! Live the life you've imagined."

It takes an enormous amount of courage to live the way Thoreau lived. He was likely a peculiar sort to the men and women of his time. While my external world may appear big and noisy to most, I live my life rather simply, deliberately, quietly. I am almost always amazed by people who are amazed by this. Thoreau's life influenced me deeply and laid a foundation on which I would pattern my own. While I have achieved some success in my life, I mostly think of myself as a modern day philosopher, a lifelong learner who yearns to make her simple life simpler still. Incidentally, today, I write to you from Thoreau's alma mater, Harvard University, where I will receive my Master's in — wait for it — education! I have settled on marrying this discipline with my work in media and entertainment. A vibrant, unorthodox but simple life was precisely the life I imagined for myself years ago in English class.

I am grateful for Henry David Thoreau and am better off because he lived.

The Writer's Retreat at Thoreau Farm, birthplace of Henry David Thoreau

The Writer's Retreat
at Thoreau Farm

"Write while the heat is in you. The writer who postpones the recording of his thoughts uses an iron which has cooled.... He cannot inflame the minds of his audience."
— Henry David Thoreau, *Journal*, February 10, 1852

Pen your masterpiece in the very room where author, philosopher, and environmentalist Henry David Thoreau was born and soak up the influential author's literary vibe in "the birthplace of ideas."

The Thoreau birthplace Writer's Retreat is the perfect country setting for writers who want uninterrupted concentration and a reprieve from urban stress. Thoreau Farm is a 295-year-old colonial New England farmhouse, adjacent to a twenty-acre organic farm in Concord, Massachusetts. Quiet fields and woods surround the house and provide inspiration through every window. In this room, in this house, Thoreau was born on July 12, 1817, where, his friend Ellery Channing wrote, "he first saw the light" and "drew his first breath in a pure country air, out of crowded towns, amid the pleasant russet fields."

Of all the 19th-century literary luminaries associated with Concord — Emerson, Hawthorne, Sidney, the Alcotts, and others — Thoreau was the only one actually born in the town. His birthplace is located close to other beloved Concord literary landmarks connected to the author and his fellow Transcendentalists, including Walden Pond, Emerson House, Orchard House, The Old Manse, and Sleepy Hollow Cemetery.

The historic house and its immediate surroundings have been restored to Thoreau's time. The site is listed on the National Register of Historic Places and won a 2012 Massachusetts Preservation Award. The comfortably furnished second floor Thoreau birth room serves as the inspirational heart of the Writer's Retreat, where you can write at a replica of the desk Thoreau used at Walden Pond.

The space is available Monday-Friday (no weekends) May-October, and seven days a week November-April. Rates are $150 per day. Payment can be made by check or Paypal. Transportation, lodging, and meals are not included, but several historic inns and restaurants are located nearby. Wifi is provided.

All rental fees support the preservation of this historic site, as well as Thoreau Farm's educational programs and outreach.

Time in our inspiring writing studio also makes an unforgettable gift for the writer in your life. Don't wait — make your reservation today!

Email us at info@thoreaufarm.org to book your date.